The Uses of
Countertransference

The Uses of
Countertransference

Michael Gorkin, Ph.D.

Jason Aronson Inc.

Northvale, New Jersey
London

10 9 8 7 6 5 4 3 2 1

The author gratefully acknowledges permission to reprint, in slightly revised form, certain of his prior publications:

Chapter 5: From "Varieties of Sexualized Countertransference," *Psychoanalytic Review*, 72:421–440, 1985. Reprinted by permission of Guilford Press.

Chapter 6: From "On the Suicide of One's Patient," *Bulletin of the Menninger Clinic*, 49:1–9, 1985. Reprinted by permission of the Bulletin of the Menninger Clinic.

Chapter 8: From "Countertransference in Cross-Cultural Psychotherapy: An Example of Jewish Therapist and Arab Patient," *Psychiatry*, 49:69–79, 1986. Reprinted by permission of Psychiatry.

Library of Congress Cataloging-in-Publication Data

Gorkin, Michael.
    The uses of countertransference.

    Includes bibliographies and index.
    1. Countertransference (Psychology)   I. Title.
[DNLM: 1. Countertransference (Psychology)
WM 62 G669u]
RC489.C68G67   1987   616.89'4   87-1068
ISBN 0-87668-970-5

Manufactured in the United States of America.

In memory of Jess Gorkin,
  my father and first editor

And for Dorothy Gorkin,
  my mother and first teacher

Contents

Acknowledgments

There are three writers whose work on countertransference has had special meaning to me: Heinrich Racker and Harold F. Searles, both courageous pioneers and early advocates of the usefulness of countertransference; and Larry Epstein, an inspirational teacher who led the seminar on countertransference at the Adelphi University Postdoctoral Program where I received my analytic training. The various references to their work, which appear throughout this book, only begin to attest to the enormous intellectual debt I owe these individuals.

A further debt of gratitude is owed to another group, who appear in the book unnamed or with a mere (and incorrect) initial—the patients and supervisees whom it has been my good fortune to work with and know. My gratitude to them extends well beyond this book.

Finally, I want to thank those at Jason Aronson Inc. who collaborated in this effort—above all, Dr. Jason Aronson, the publisher; Lori Williams, Production Editor; and Nancy Morgan Andreola, the copyeditor. They did what every writer hopes for: They helped me write this book in the best way I could. I am deeply grateful to them for it.

1

The Expanding Definition

There are few terms in the psychoanalytic lexicon that over time have proved more elusive or generated more ideological controversy than the term *countertransference*. This chapter will outline how this definitional clash arose, as well as some of the principal directions it has taken. To be included are a discussion of Freud's view of counter-transference; some early embellishments of Freud's defi-nition; the "challenge" of the late 1940s and early 1950s, which sought to broaden radically the concept of counter-transference; and some of the more recent paths this skirmish has taken. My purpose here is to sketch this history in broad strokes, rather than to present a review of the literature, a task which has been sensitively accom-plished by Orr (1954), Kernberg (1965), Langs (1976a), and Ernsberger (1979).

Freud's View of Countertransference

In all of Freud's writings, there is not one full discussion
of countertransference. In fact, his explicit reference to
the topic was limited to two published writings. The first
of these is the address that Freud delivered in 1910 to a
congress of his colleagues in Nuremberg on the topic "The
Future Prospects of Psycho-Analytic Therapy." It was
here that he introduced the term *countertransference*
(*gugenübertragung*), in words that were cautionary, and
even forbidding. He stated: "We have become aware of
the 'counter-transference,' which arises in him [the physi-
cian] as a result of the patient's influence on his unconscious feelings, and we are almost inclined to insist that he
shall recognize this counter-transference in himself and
overcome it" (1910, pp. 144–145).

Freud's second explicit reference to countertransference was in his 1915 paper, "Observations on Transfer-
ence-Love." While less forbidding in tone, Freud was
again cautioning his (male) colleagues on the dangers of
responding countertransferentially to the transference
love of their (female) patients. Freud wrote: "Our control
over ourselves is not so complete that we may not suddenly one day go further than we intended. In my opinion,
therefore, we ought not to give up the neutrality towards
the patient, which we have acquired through keeping the
counter-transference in check" (1915, p. 164).

In neither the 1910 nor the 1915 paper does Freud
present a well-honed definition of countertransference.
This lack of precision on Freud's part has led to some
confusion and difference of opinion as to what he meant
by the term. Did he mean that countertransference was
strictly the analyst's transference or, more broadly, did it
comprise all of the analyst's conflict-laden reactions to the

patient? Or did he mean that it was a "counter" to the patient's transference, in which case it might also include realistic responses to the patient's transference to him? Most investigators argue (and I would agree) that Freud equated countertransference with the analyst's transference, or with other conflict-laden reactions to the patient.

If Freud's definition of countertransference is not altogether clear, it is nonetheless apparent that he used the term in a pejorative manner. Countertransference was a hindrance, to be kept "in check" or to be "overcome." It interfered with the analyst's necessary neutrality, his ability to listen to his patient with neither fear, nor distemper, nor desire. As Freud envisioned it, a central function of the analyst's training analysis was to help him work through his neurotic problems and thereby reduce potential areas of countertransferential difficulty. Freud did not specify to what extent he believed it was actually possible to eliminate countertransference-based reactions from impinging on the treatment. Yet one gathers from his comments (1937) on the interminability of analysis, and from his suggestions that analysts return periodically for more analysis, that he considered countertransferential brushfires a hazard of the trade. It was left to the moral and professional integrity of the analyst to see to it that these brushfires caused as little damage as possible.

Early Departures from Freud's Concept

While the principal challenge to Freud's notion of countertransference did not appear until some 40 years after he coined the term, there were still some important rumblings of disagreement in the intervening years. This early dissent made it apparent that at issue was no less than a controversy over how psychoanalysis cured, and what role the analyst played in the cure. The significance or irrelevance of the analyst as a "real" person, the degree of advisable emotional involvement of the analyst with the patient, the role of interpretation versus new experience in the curative process—all these matters, still in debate today, tended to find their way into the controversy over the nature of countertransference and its role in the analytic process.

The first significant embellishment of Freud's notion of countertransference came from his friend, former analysand, and member of the Freudian inner circle: Ferenczi. As part of his "active" technique, Ferenczi (1920, 1925, 1931, 1933) gradually came to view countertransference, and especially the technical uses of countertransference, in a manner quite different from that proposed by Freud. Ferenczi did not wage his disagreements in terms of a debate over the definition of countertransference. But as he developed his technical approach of interacting with the patient in an emotional, direct way—in part, with the conscious aim of reparenting the patient—Ferenczi used his emotional reactions in ways that, at times, veered radically from the Freudian framework.

Ferenczi believed that the analyst's actual feelings, blind spots, and neurotic vestiges were intuitively known to the patient, and that they played a greater role in the treatment, for good or ill, than Freud had indicated. In addition, he advocated the occasional disclosure of these feelings and attitudes to the patient (1931, p. 133; 1933, p. 159). Sometimes, when caught up in a countertransference-based error, he would even go so far as to "enter into extensive free association as to [his] unconscious motives in making the error" (Thompson 1943, p. 65). None of these technical measures was accepted by Freud, nor by the mainstream of his followers, and they contributed to the painful break that took place between the two men during the 1920s.

Ferenczi, however, as founder of the Hungarian Psycho-Analytical Society, had his own group of pupils and adherents. Some of their work amplified and extended Ferenczi's views, and as such, challenged Freud's approach to countertransference. Perhaps the best known of Ferenczi's pupils was his translator and literary executor, M. Balint. Later known for his work on preoedipal disorders and the "basic fault," Balint, along with his wife, wrote an early paper, "On Transference and Countertransference" (1939), which clearly reflected Ferenczi's influence. Echoing Ferenczi, the Balints pointed to the inevitable intrusion of the analyst's personality in the analytic setting. From the smallest detail of office decor to the manner and form of delivering interpretations, the analyst's character and transference enter into the relationship with the patient. In a statement which has since become a rallying cry, the Balints concluded: "Looked at from this point of view the analytical situation is the result of an interplay between the patient's transference and the analyst's countertransference, complicated by the reactions released in each by the other's transference to him" (p. 228).

Other pupils of Ferenczi also amplified the Freudian view of countertransference. The most radical, and perhaps most unswerving, of Ferenczi's followers was DeForest. In a paper entitled "The Therapeutic Technique of Sandor Ferenczi" (1942), she underscored the interactive quality of transference and countertransference, and discussed her own frequent use of countertransference experiences with patients. In addition, she suggested a perspective on countertransference that has since been assumed by a number of analysts—namely, the importance of the analyst's receptivity to the patient's communications about the intrusion of countertransference material. She stated: "It is probable that the analyst's sincere evaluation of his own personality and a willingness to learn from his patient of his own short-comings, changing them when possible, are among the most essential elements in the development of the patient's growing reality sense, his tolerance, and his capacity to bear disappointment" (p. 134).

While Ferenczi and his followers were sowing some seeds of controversy on one side of the Atlantic, on the other side a singular American was reworking the psychoanalytic garden in his own distinctive manner. Sullivan, founder of the "interpersonal" school, staunchly disagreed, like Ferenczi and his followers, with Freud's notion of the analyst as neutral observer. He simply did not believe such a role was possible. Sullivan believed, rather, that the analyst related to the patient not only as an observer, but also as a participant. The analyst's personality and transferences were inevitably drawn into the interaction. Sullivan was less sanguine than was Ferenczi about the curative value of the analyst's emotional responses to the patient. Like Freud, Sullivan tended to emphasize the potential negative impact of the analyst's emotional responses. He did not debate Freud's definition of countertransference. Yet, by reframing the entire interaction between analyst and patient, he indicated—more radically than had Ferenczi—that the transference-countertransference interplay was part of the ongoing therapeutic process. In so doing, Sullivan established a theory of treatment that would soon be used by his followers to reformulate and reevaluate the Freudian concept of countertransference.

While both Sullivan and Ferenczi were quite aware of their opposition to Freud, another theorist who contributed to extending the notion of countertransference seemingly did so with little awareness of her original contribution. In 1926, Deutsch published a paper inauspiciously entitled "Occult Processes Occurring During Psychoanalysis." In this paper, she indicated that countertransference may serve a useful purpose. In particular, she discussed two types of countertransference: (1) identifications with the patient's infantile strivings; and (2) the "complementary attitude"—the identifications with the (transference) objects of these strivings. Deutsch acknowledged that these identifications could become a hindrance in the treatment. For the analyst who had sufficiently worked through his infantile conflicts, however, these identifications, acting on an unconscious level, provided the constructive basis for his "intuitive empathy." She summarized: "The utilization and goal-directed mastery of this countertransference are some of the most important duties of the analyst" (p. 137).

Deutsch did not delineate how these unconscious identifications were elicited or induced in the analyst. She lacked at the time the metapsychological tools to amplify her notions. I also suspect that she was not aware of the importance of her contributions to the theoretical discussion of countertransference. Little attention was given to her paper upon its publication. It was not until some two decades later that her notions were more fully developed—above all by Racker, who employed her ideas in his elaborate discussion of "concordant" and "complementary" countertransferences.

Broadening the Definition: The "Challenge" of the Late 1940s and Early 1950s

Apart from the work of Sullivan, Ferenczi, and a few others, there was little attempt among psychoanalysts to

explore the territory of the analyst's emotional responsiveness to the patient. The mainstream position continued to be the highly cautious view handed down by
Freud. The analyst was expected to react outwardly *and*
inwardly to the patient in a "neutral" manner. Any disturbance of these still waters of analytic neutrality was considered a hindrance to the treatment and a reflection of
unresolved, unconscious conflicts in the analyst. The ultimate remedy was more analysis for the analyst. The immediate remedy was to transfer the patient.

     This stance, and all that it implied, was to receive its
stiffest "challenge" in the late 1940s and early 1950s. In a
rash of articles appearing in the leading psychoanalytic
journals, a number of analysts—representing principally
the British object relations school and the Sullivanian
interpersonal school—attacked the Freudian approach to
countertransference. In their cumulative impact, these
investigations challenged the prevailing concept of countertransference in a manner that could no longer be ig-
nored (even if not accepted) by the mainstream of psychoanalysis.

     To understand the timing of this challenge, it is
helpful to examine some of the trends of the time both
within the psychoanalytic community (or communities)
and within the larger societies in which psychoanalysis
was practiced. I am not sure what weight to attach to each
of the various trends, but it seems likely that they reinforced one another and contributed to a notable change
of atmosphere in some analytic circles. For instance,
the controversy over the role of the analyst in general,
and of countertransference in particular, would seem to
have been influenced by a significant shift in the larger
society(ies) toward a democratization of social structures.
The society in which psychoanalysis was spawned—pre-

World War I Europe—was a far more authoritarian matrix than were the societies in which psychoanalysis was
practiced at the midcentury. The social changes of the
previous 40 years had rendered it such that authority no
longer went unchallenged, be that authority the leader of
the country, the father in the family, or the doctor in the
office: Where authority was not under attack, it was at
least under scrutiny. This trend also impinged on the
psychoanalytic community. In short, I do not think it was
mere chance that in this changing social milieu, the analyst, benign authority that he professed to be, also came
under closer examination. (A more elaborate argument
along these lines can be found in Szasz 1956.)*

Further contributing to the closer examination of the
analyst's role in the psychoanalytic situation was a trend
that affected science in general. The notion of an objective, mechanical observer—the "neutral" observer, in
Freud's terms—was called into question on epistemologi-
cal grounds. For even in a science as exact as physics, it
was argued by Heisenberg and Einstein that the act of
observation or the position of the observer influences the
nature of the data that are gathered. How then could an
analyst, observing the far less exact data of the patient's
productions, expect to be objective, to be uninfluenced by
the nature of these data? This argument carried particular
weight for Sullivan and his followers, and provided a
philosophical underpinning for their approach—namely,
that the analyst's and patient's reactions make up a single
"field" and cannot be thought of in isolation. From this it
followed that countertransference could not go unscrutin-
ized.

---

*I think it is possible to understand the challenge to Freud as also
emanating, in part, from this general trend.

In addition to these two influences of a social and philosophical nature, there were important trends within the psychoanalytic community itself that abetted the greater exploration of countertransference. In the years between Freud's initial pronouncements on countertransference and the challenge of the midcentury, there had been a growing emphasis on preoedipal development and preoedipal disorders. This shift quite obviously brought the child's relationship to the preoedipal mother into much sharper focus. For many analysts, one outcome of this shift was a tendency to see the analyst–patient dyad increasingly in terms of the mother–child dyad; this was especially true with more disturbed patients. Thus, just as one could not talk about what was happening inside the child without exploring what was happening inside the mother, so by analogy it made little sense to talk about what was happening inside the patient without reference to what was happening inside the analyst. This argument, in one form or another, was implicit in the work of a number of investigators representing the British object relations school and the interpersonal school.

A final influence leading to the greater examination of countertransference data and their meaning was one that is often referred to as "the widening scope of psychoanalysis"—that is, more seriously disturbed patients were supposedly entering psychoanalytic treatment. I am not sure this is true, and in any case there is no way of verifying it. But what is undoubtedly true is that these more deeply disturbed patients, in whatever numbers they arrived, generated more chronic and chaotic countertransference reactions than did neurotics, and it gradually became clear that the management and resolution of these countertransferences was central to the therapy in these cases. Little wonder, then, that among those investigators who sought to broaden the Freudian concept of counter-transference were several who had worked at length with severely impaired, preoedipal patients.

Having cited these trends which, in their various and cumulative ways, contributed to the outpouring of interest in countertransference issues in the late 1940s and early 1950s, I wish to turn now to some of the pivotal investigators of that period, highlighting the ways in which their contributions extended the notion of counter-transference as both a theoretical and technical concept. Again, my aim is not to provide a review of the literature. The reader who is interested in a more detailed review will find useful the work of Langs (1976a) and Ernsberger (1979).

As one surveys the literature that, taken as a whole, comprises the "challenge" of the late 1940s and early 1950s, it becomes clear that this challenge was more than simply a definitional dispute over the term *countertransference*. To be sure, there was a tendency among many investigators to define more precisely the domain of counter-transference—a tendency which led one investigator (Little 1957) to lament, "Our difficulty here is to get one word not to mean as many different things as there are people using it" (p. 240). Yet, what was at stake in this linguistic squabble was a problem that went to the heart of psychoanalytic technique: What was the expectable and desirable stance of the analyst vis-à-vis the patient? How emotionally involved should the analyst be in the treatment of a patient? Or, otherwise put, was analytic neutrality a feasible, or even worthwhile, aim? And if so, was it so with all patients—psychotics (today, we would add border-lines) as well as neurotics?

With these crucial technical issues at stake, it is perhaps not surprising that the debate over countertrans-

ference was a feisty and fervent one. What Ferenczi and
his followers had begun, midcentury writers sought to
continue. They did so at times with a certain polemical
quality, but also with a greater sophistication and sweep
than before. In the matter of a half-dozen years, 1947 to
1953, they elevated the topic of countertransference from
the basement to the main floor of psychoanalytic discussion, where it has remained ever since, even if the issues
raised then still occasion widespread and heated disagreement.

The British Object Relations School:
Heimann, Winnicott, Little, Racker

If one had to identify a single article of that period as most
fully representing the challenge, it would have to be Heimann's concise (four page) and articulate statement, "On
Counter-Transference," which appeared in 1950. (It had
been read the previous year at the International Psychoanalytic Congress in Zurich.) Broadly and boldly, Heimann stated her argument, which also became the theme
of others.

> I have been struck by the widespread belief among
> candidates that the counter-transference is nothing
> but a source of trouble. Many candidates are afraid
> and feel guilty when they become aware of feelings
> towards their patients and consequently aim at avoid-
> ing any emotional response and at becoming com-
> pletely unfeeling and "detached." . . . My thesis is
> that the analyst's emotional response to his patient
> within the analytic situation represents one of the
> most important tools for his work. The analyst's
> counter-transference is an instrument of research
> into the patient's unconscious [p. 81].

From this plain rebuttal of the prevailing Freudian approach to countertransference, Heimann expanded her thesis. In developing her view of countertransference as a potentially useful tool, she adumbrated two notions that have since received enormous attention: (1) the concept of a predictable emotional response on the part of the therapist to the patient's transference; and (2) the notion that this predictable response may be explained in part by the influence of the patient's actively projecting aspects of himself onto the therapist (a view that has been elaborated in subsequent work on projective identification).

In underscoring the importance of the analyst's emotional responsiveness, Heimann radically expanded the definition of countertransference to include all of the analyst's feelings and fantasies about the patient. She became the leading proponent of what Kernberg (1965) has called the "totalistic" view of countertransference (as opposed to the "classical" view). Such a sweeping definition of countertransference had obvious problems, for unless one is prepared to categorize all of the patient's feelings and fantasies toward the therapist as transference, it would seem to make little linguistic sense to subsume all of the therapist's reactions under the rubric of countertransference. Although she anticipated and acknowledged this conceptual problem, Heimann did not attempt to resolve it. She was more concerned with technical issues than theoretical ones and was apparently eager to sidestep definitional niceties.

She did take care, nevertheless, to stress that she was not advocating a freewheeling, overt, emotional exchange between therapist and patient. To be useful, the therapist's emotional reaction should be under control, not too intense. She wrote: "Since, however, violent emotions of any kind, of love or hate, helpfulness or anger, impel towards action rather than towards contemplation and blur a person's capacity to observe and weigh evidence correctly, it follows that, if the analyst's emotional response is intense, it will defeat its object" (p. 82). Moreover, the sole purpose of the analyst's emotional reactivity was to gather information. "I do not," she wrote, "consider it right for the analyst to communicate his feelings to his patient. In my view such honesty is more in the nature of a confession and a burden to the patient" (p. 83).

In addition to Heimann's pointed attack on the classical view of countertransference, there is another paper of that era that has since proved equally seminal and, in its own way, more fundamentally radical—Winnicott's "Hate in the Countertransference." It was first read to the British Psycho-Analytical Society in 1947 and subsequently published in 1949. Years later, Winnicott, in a brief aside, noted that his 1947/1949 paper was actually meant to be more about hate than about countertransference (1960, p. 17). Be that as it may, subsequent researchers have paid considerable attention to the paper's radical commentary on the meaning and uses of certain countertransferential data.

In distinguishing between various types of countertransference phenomena, Winnicott differentiated the therapist's conflict-laden responses from what he called "the truly objective countertransference"—in other words, "the analyst's love and hate in reaction to the actual personality of the patient, based on objective observation" (1949, p. 70). This was the first use of the term *objective countertransference*. Winnicott did not refine this notion, nor did he suggest, as Heimann did soon after, that different kinds of patients might be expected to evoke different types of expectable countertransferences. He was writing about one type of expectable reaction and one broad category of patients: specifically, the analyst's hatred as it was predictably evoked by very disturbed patients, such as those with psychoses and antisocial personalities. This was a controversial notion. Nobody before had stated so clearly that the analyst could be expected to hate certain patients. What made the paper all the more radical was that Winnicott argued both for the advisability of revealing, albeit in modulated form, the nature of one's hatred to the patient, and for the analyst's need to do so not only for the patient's sake, but also to enable himself to endure and carry out the treatment. It is curious that Winnicott, master technician that he was, never went on to elaborate these provocative technical ideas. In fact, when he again addressed the subject of countertransference years later (1960), he reverted to the classical definition of the term, apparently dismissing his earlier terminology of *objective countertransference* (though not the technical content to which this terminology applied).

Winnicott's original work, however, had an immediate impact on his colleagues. One of these, Little—who also became an analysand of Winnicott's during this period—was to expand and elaborate upon Winnicott's ideas. She, too, was fundamentally interested in the analyst's use of his emotional reactions in work with seriously disturbed patients. She staked out her position in two poignant, heartfelt papers: "Counter-transference and the Patient's Response to It" (1951), and an expansion of that work, "'R'—The Analyst's Total Response to His Patient's Needs" (1957). While generally accepting the "classical" definition of countertransference (though she sometimes wavered between "classical" and "totalistic" definitions), she nonetheless remained the most radical proponent of the use of countertransference. She believed that in working with the severely disturbed patient, the therapist must remain open to experiencing all sorts of

intense emotional reactions to the patient, many of which
will necessarily reflect the therapist's own unresolved conflicts. In order to make clear to the patient one's genuineness and honesty, and in order to render the patient more
accepting of his own transferences, one must at times
disclose the nature of one's countertransference distortions.

   Little minced no words in stating this technical advice, and at times she waxed downright polemical. She
wrote: "Analysts often behave unconsciously exactly like
the parents who put up a smoke-screen, and tantalize their
children, tempting them to see the very things they forbid
their seeing; and not to refer to counter-transference is
tantamount to denying its existence, or forbidding the
patient to know or speak about it" (1951, p. 38). Little was
not altogether clear as to when she disclosed countertransference (in the narrow "classical" sense or, more widely,
in the sense of "objective" reactions as well), nor was she
clear about just how self-disclosing one ought to be. One
gathers that she varied her dosing of countertransferential
data from patient to patient and in the course of the
treatment of any given patient; she indicated, for example,
that she is more likely to be self-revealing later in the
analysis than when the analysis is in its earlier stages.
Furthermore, in agreement with DeForest, and anticipat-
ing such later writers as Searles and Langs, she stated that
the patient will often provide useful interpretations to the
analyst about his countertransference. In such cases, therapy may be a two-way street. In sum, Little's principal
contribution to the countertransference literature was not
in her reworking or refining of the concept of countertransference, but in her bold approach to the analyst's
technical use of his emotional reactions to the patient.

   An investigator who did attempt to rework and refine

the theoretical concept of countertransference, and whose classification of these reactions is the most far-reaching we have to date, is the Argentinean, Racker. I have included him with the British object relations school because his work is so clearly steeped in Kleinian theory and terminology. In fact, I suspect that, had Racker cast his ideas on countertransference in terminology that was less frankly Kleinian, these ideas might have won him an even wider audience.

Racker's two most influential papers are "A Contribution to the Problem of Counter-Transference," which was delivered to the Argentine Psychoanalytic Association in 1948 and published in English in 1953, and "The Meanings and Uses of Countertransference," delivered to the same association in 1953 and published in English in 1957. In these papers, Racker adopted a "totalistic" definition of countertransference, as did Heimann, but, unlike the latter, he carefully mapped out the various types of countertransference reactions and experiences.

Racker differentiated between *indirect* countertransference (to third parties, such as members of the patient's family, or to one's colleagues and supervisors) and *direct* countertransference (to the patient himself). In the category of direct countertransference, he further distinguished between two types of countertransference reactions. One type occurs when the analyst forms *concordant identifications*—when, for example, the analyst's ego is identified with the patient's ego, his id with the patient's id, and so on. In these situations, the analyst feels himself to be empathically in tune with the patient. For example, the patient might be rebellious toward the analyst, and the analyst might empathize with this rebellious feeling, understanding from his own past what it is like to be rebellious toward an authority. The second type of direct countertransference occurs when the analyst forms *com-plementary identifications*—that is, when the analyst finds himself identifying with an *unwanted* part of the patient's self or superego. Using the foregoing example, if instead of empathizing with the rebellious part of the patient, the analyst were to experience a judgmental and critical response toward the patient, he could be said to have taken on a complementary identification—in this case, the (patient's) superego in relation to the patient's rebellious self. In general, then, when a concordant identification (empathy) fails, a complementary identification occurs.

As Racker was quick to point out, however, complementary identifications cannot be avoided, not even in the most thoroughly analyzed and well-meaning analyst. This is so for two reasons. First, the analyst always has a "personal equation," unresolved neurotic vestiges which impel him to respond transferentially to the patient. Racker wrote: "We are still children and neurotics even when we are adults and analysts" (1957, p. 303). Second, the patient, through his projective identifications, is rather constantly inducing the therapist to experience himself in this "complementary" manner. So, as Racker envisioned it, just as the patient is led to experience a transference neurosis, the analyst will be led to experience a "countertransference neurosis"—one which corresponds in a complementary way to the patient's neurosis.

Racker systematically outlined a wide number of typical countertransference reactions—boredom, guilt, masochism, paranoia—which he traced to specific transferences of the patient. What Heimann had alluded to in her brief comments about predictable countertransference reactions, Racker fully delineated. He did so in such profuse detail that he has been accused at times of a mechanistic approach. I do not share this criticism. I believe

Racker was pointing to the likelihood of the development of certain countertransferential reactions and countertransferential neuroses, but their precise form and intensity is always, in part, dependent on who the particular analyst is, on his "personal equation." Racker was especially cautious about what the analyst should do with countertransference. He was certain that countertransference could be employed in understanding the patient and, more than anyone before or since, he presented a case for the informational value of countertransference. Yet he left as an open question whether the communication of some countertransference reactions was of therapeutic use to the patient.

The Sullivanian Interpersonal School: Fromm-Reichmann, Cohen

The contribution of the interpersonal school to the challenge of the late 1940s and early 1950s was, on the whole, less far-reaching and influential than that of the British object relations school. Several papers were written by Sullivan's followers; interestingly, they were far less polemical in tone than some of the early papers of the British object relations school. The latter, after all, had an axe to grind with many of their Freudian colleagues. The interpersonalists, on the other hand, were merely refining the work of Sullivan who, in axiomatic fashion, had asserted that transference *and* countertransference (parataxic distortions, as he called them) were bound to infuse the ongoing interchange between patient and therapist.

Probably the best known of the early interpersonalists who addressed the matter of countertransference is Fromm-Reichmann. In her influential text *Principles of Intensive Psychotherapy* (1950) and in subsequent papers

such as "Clinical Significance of Intuitive Processes of the
Psychoanalyst" (1955), Fromm-Reichmann made it clear
that she considered countertransference a useful tool for
understanding the patient. She wrote: "The psychiatrist
who is trained in the observation and inner realization of
his reaction to patients' manifestations can frequently
utilize these reactions as a helpful instrument in understanding otherwise hidden implications in patients' communications" (1950, pp. 5–6).

In general, Fromm-Reichmann seemed to favor a totalistic definition of countertransference, and in the tradition of Ferenczi, as well as Little and Racker, she alluded
to a *positive countertransference*, by which she meant,
broadly, the therapist's empathic emotional involvement
with the patient. Although she did not make a special
point that the therapist might profitably disclose certain
countertransferences, several of her case examples make it
clear that she was at times quite self-revealing in her work
with some psychotic patients. She argued, moreover, that
the patient can sometimes provide the therapist with the
clearest interpretation of his countertransferences. In
sum, Fromm-Reichmann presented a more precise notion
of countertransference than did Sullivan, but one which
was firmly within the interpersonal framework. As such, it
challenged, rather matter-of-factly, the classical Freudian
view.

Another Sullivanian whose work sought to redefine
the notion of countertransference was Cohen. Her paper
"Countertransference and Anxiety" (1952) was an effort
to recast the definition of countertransference in terms of
a theory of anxiety. Her definition: "When, in the patient–analyst relationship, anxiety is aroused in the analyst with the effect that communication between the two is
interfered with by some alteration in the analyst's behav-

ior, verbal or otherwise, then countertransference is present" (p. 235).

It might seem at first glance that Cohen's definition implies that countertransference is a hindrance to the treatment process, and that she is thus assuming a more Freudian view. In fact, she attempted to demonstrate just the opposite. She argued that countertransference—and hence, anxiety in the therapist—occurs rather frequently in the course of treatment. The anxiety may be conscious, or it may be kept submerged by the therapist's defenses. In general, the therapist's anxiety is caused by situational factors in the therapist's life, or by the therapist's unresolved neurotic problems, or by the communication of the patient's anxiety to the therapist. Her examples indicate that countertransferences are often composed of a mixture of these factors. In a manner consonant with Racker's formulations, Cohen argued that the well-analyzed therapist (in Racker's terms, the therapist who knows his personal equation) can often extrapolate from his own attitudes and defensive maneuvers the patient's role in the interpersonal situation—that is, the patient's role in evoking anxiety in the therapist. Cohen abstained from answering the question of what the therapist ought to disclose of the countertransference, but she was firm in her belief that countertransferential data can provide some of the most useful clues as to what is occurring in the treatment.

Interestingly, Cohen's redefinition of countertransference did not catch on. This may be so both on the practical grounds that she did not define explicitly enough the specific types of countertransferential reactions, and also on the metapsychological grounds that analysts were then, and continue to be, less focused on anxiety per se than on the forces which give rise to anxiety (id and superego tensions, or self-object representations) and on the elaboration of these forces in the therapeutic exchange. In retrospect, then, it was Cohen's conclusions as to the usefulness of countertransference which proved noteworthy, and not so much the route she took to arrive at these conclusions.

Freudian Contributions: Weigert, Gitelson, Berman

In addition to the interpersonalists and British object relations analysts, there were some voices within the Freudian establishment that contributed to the challenge. These voices tended to be cautious, and the challenge was presented with due care so as not to offend the sensibilities of their orthodox colleagues. Quotations from Freud, especially those which demonstrated his "human" side, were marshalled in as evidence that these new ideas about countertransference were not so much deviations as logical extensions of The Tradition. These papers, in my view, offered less to the discussion than the work of the British object relations school. Yet the mere fact that they were being written at all indicated that the Freudian notion of countertransference was, even in the most traditional places, at last being scrutinized.

In three papers written during this period, Weigert (1952, 1954a, 1954b) outlined some theoretical and technical revisions to the more restricted Freudian view of countertransference. She stated her thesis as follows: "I cannot agree with a definition of countertransference which emphasizes only its negative character. It is true, as long as countertransference remains unconscious, that it may function as a hindrance to the analytic process. But since we assume the analyst's continuous self-analysis during his work, I would like to suggest a definition of countertransference which acknowledges the valuable insight that we gain from it" (1952, p. 472). In her totalistic definition of countertransference, Weigert also included the notion of a "sensitive" or "empathic" countertransference. By this she meant that the analyst may identify consciously with both the patient and the patient's objects, and in so doing is able to use the emotional reactions as a source of information about the patient and the nature of his transferences (1952, p. 474; 1954a, p. 243). Weigert did not believe that the analyst should reveal countertransferences to the patient until the terminal phase of treatment. Only then, when transferences and related countertransferences have lost their quality of *sturm und drang*, can the analyst afford to be more self-revealing without his disclosures' impinging on the development of the patient's transferences. Weigert indicated, however, that such a terminal phase is not frequently reached in actual clinical practice.

An orthodox analyst who espoused a more open disclosure of countertransference was Gitelson, who wrote a rather widely quoted paper, "The Emotional Position of the Analyst in the Psycho-Analytic Situation" (1952), a version of which had been read to the American Psychoanalytic Association in 1949. Gitelson's definition of countertransference was somewhat idiosyncratic, although it fit well within the classical Freudian framework. He defined countertransference as the analyst's reactions to "partial aspects" of the patient—specifically, the patient's transference, or material brought by the patient to the treatment, or the patient's reactions to the analyst as a person. Gitelson envisioned these countertransferences as occurring once treatment was well underway and, further, as hindering the treatment. Idiosyncratically, he did not include the analyst's transferences in his notion of countertransference. He saw these transferences as "reactions to the patient as a whole," and as occurring at the outset of treatment. These distinctions were generally regarded as arbitrary (Cohen 1952, Kernberg 1965), inasmuch as "whole" reactions—that is, the analyst's transferences— by no means occur only in the initial phase of treatment. In fact, some of the examples that Gitelson frankly provided as demonstrations of his own countertransferences would clearly be considered as emanating from his transference distortions. Yet what made Gitelson's contribution of interest, in my view, was his candid handling of his countertransferences as they impinged on treatment. He suggested that ". . . the analyst may reveal as much of himself as is needed to foster and support the patient's testing of reality" (p. 8). While this statement was open to interpretation, Gitelson made it clear that he believed countertransferences to be unavoidable and recurrent during any treatment. Moreover, his case vignettes suggest that he was more self-disclosing at these times than many of his Freudian colleagues.

Another analyst who contributed to the broadening approach toward countertransference was Berman. Berman's definition of countertransference as the analyst's transference was clearly within the classical camp. But in discussing some of the analyst's "attitudes" toward the patient, he veered from most of his orthodox colleagues. His paper "Countertransference and Attitudes of the Analyst in the Therapeutic Process," which was read to the American Psychoanalytic Association in 1948 and published in revised form in the Sullivanian journal *Psychiatry* in 1949, has a definite interpersonal "feel" to it. Gone is any pretense of the "neutral" analyst; instead, the analyst is seen as emotionally involved with the patient. Berman stated: ". . . the analytic situation is, in a sense, a personal one for the analyst, and most if not all patients either dimly sense this fact or have occasion to observe it quite directly. It seems to be disturbing to realize and face fully how cathected, and sometimes highly cathected, the patient and his analysis may be for the analyst" (p. 160).

Berman pointed out that some of the analyst's "attitudes" are evoked by the patient's behavior and transferences. Significantly, he did not take the additional step of suggesting, as did others, that the analyst can use these evoked reactions in understanding the patient. Had he done so, his paper might have had a wider and more enduring impact. Berman did take another interesting and somewhat iconoclastic step, however—one which is also suggested in the work of Winnicott and Little. He argued that the analyst's struggle with his own emotional reactions and "attitudes" serves a vital curative function in the treatment. The analyst need not disclose this struggle; the patient will be aware of it and will experience it as part of the analyst's "dedication" to him. Berman wrote: "I think it is in the *process* through which the analyst under stress achieves realistic and well-integrated functioning that an important therapeutic factor is to be found" (p. 164). Berman indicated that what is curative here is, in part, the new experience of the patient with the therapist. Thus, despite his classical definition of countertransference and his cautious approach toward self-disclosure, Berman, in his discussion of the analyst's emotional reactions to the patient, was advocating an analytic stance that differed from the classical Freudian view, and in this way he contributed to the multifaceted challenge of the time.

The Classical Response to the Challenge: Reich

As previously indicated, the challenge of the late 1940s and early 1950s to the classical view of countertransference was a multidimensional one. Various contributors disagreed in one manner or another with Freud's conceptions. Before proceeding to the classical response to the challenge, it may be useful to summarize the principal revisions that emerged during this period.

In brief, the classical concept of countertransference had been judged and found wanting. No longer was there solid agreement that the term *countertransference* ought to apply to the analyst's principally unconscious, conflict-ridden reactions. Some analysts had begun to talk of positive or empathic countertransferences, while others began to distinguish between countertransferences that are due primarily to the analyst's conflicts, and those that are predictable, "objective." With the broadened application of the term came an expanded sense that countertransferences need not be only a hindrance; they could be useful, providing information about the patient. Widespread disagreement remained among these revisionists over what, if anything, could be disclosed to the patient, although it was evident that some analysts—particularly in their work with more disturbed patients—were practicing rather open and bold self-disclosure. Beyond all this, there had occurred an undeniable shift in atmosphere that affected *all* analysts. Simply put, analysts of all persuasions seemed to become more cognizant of their emotional reactions to their patients, and more aware that these reactions entered regularly into the analytic situation in one way or another. And this was true whether one referred to these reactions as countertransference per se, or by some other name.

The classical response in the decade following the challenge was articulated by a number of investigators, the most outspoken of whom was Reich. In two papers, "On Countertransference" (1951) and "Further Remarks on Countertransference" (1960), Reich offered a reaffirmation of Freud's 1910/1915 concept of countertransference—a reaffirmation which she stated in more exacting detail and with more fervid conviction.

Reich's definition of countertransference is a well-honed version of Freud's original concept. For her, the term may be defined narrowly to mean the analyst's transference to the patient or, more broadly, to include additional conflict-laden, and principally unconscious, reactions of the analyst to the patient (1951, p. 26). Reich regarded conscious reactions as countertransferences only if inordinately intense or clearly of a sexual or aggressive nature, in which case, she argued, they invariably are determined by unconscious infantile strivings (1960, p. 390).

Reich was most astute in delineating a wide spectrum of countertransferential attitudes (in her definition) that the analyst sometimes brings into the treatment situation. In fact, her initial paper on countertransference, written when the challenge was just beginning, was primarily a discussion of the litany of countertransferential pitfalls that beset analysts: sexual, aggressive, guilt-ridden, phobic and counterphobic, narcissistic, and paranoid attitudes that the analyst may bring into the treatment situation. She distinguished these "permanent" attitudes from "acute" manifestations, which are more situationally determined and, she argued, more amenable to quick repair.

Her prescription for remedying the "permanent" attitudes was simply more analysis for the analyst.

With unswerving fervor, Reich reiterated the classical call for the analyst's "neutrality." For her, neutrality meant that the analyst remains an observer and at no time becomes a participant—in the sense of emotional involvement—with the patient. The analyst must remain "uninvolved" (1951, p. 25; 1960, p. 391). Any feelings toward the patient beyond a physicianly concern and a mild sense of like or dislike are prima facie evidence that some countertransferential impingement has occurred. The analyst is expected to empathize with the patient, to form "trial identifications" with him (or his objects). It was Reich's belief, however, that these trial identifications must be made in short-lived forays, *without* emotional involvement. Here she was clearly offering a rebuttal to many of the investigators who issued the challenge, and who were suggesting that emotional involvement, sometimes intense, was an unavoidable part of such empathic identifications. Reich was bitingly dismissive of those investigators who assumed a predictable or objective reaction on the part of the analyst to certain of the patient's transferences or behavior. She did not believe the analyst could in any way rely on these emotional reactions as a barometer of the patient's inner world. In a rebuttal to Winnicott, Racker, and others, she argued: "All such notions about a typical content of countertransference represent schematizations and a narrowing down of the beautiful variety of psychic functioning" (1960, p. 393).

Finally, Reich enunciated the classical view of disclosure of the countertransference (in her definition) or of any other of the analyst's personal reactions: It was not useful and it was not permissible. Such self-disclosures interfered with the development of transference and were a burden to the patient. The only exception, according to Reich, should be on those occasions when the analyst makes a frank error—forgetting something, a slip of the tongue—in which case a simple admission is deemed sufficient. She did not discuss what the analyst might do upon becoming aware of the intrusion of a long-standing countertransferential issue. One suspects her advice would be for the analyst to turn the patient over to another therapist, and turn himself in for more analysis.

In sum, Reich provided an unswerving version of Freud's original notions. Like Freud, she saw countertransference as material that needed to be kept "in check" or "overcome." Countertransferences were bound to occur, but they were a hindrance to the analytic work. She summarized this thesis in bold and succinct terms: *"The countertransference as such is not helpful but the readiness to acknowledge its existence and the ability to overcome it is"* (1960, p. 392; italics are hers).

Current Approaches to Countertransference

I think it no exaggeration to say that all further theoretical and technical refinements of the concept of countertransference stem from those seminal investigations of the late 1940s and early 1950s. That was an unusually productive period and, in a sense, we are still building on that original work. We also remain steeped in many of the controversies that emerged then, although there has been movement toward consensus on some issues.

In the last decade or so, for instance, fewer analysts, including "classical" analysts, are ascribing to Reich's view that the analyst's emotional responses to the patient are of *no* value in understanding the patient's inner world. The matter of what to call these responses—countertransference or something else—is another question, one which will be discussed next. The point here is simply that there has been a growing consensus that the analyst's emotional responses to the patient can provide useful information about the patient.

In part, this change in perspective has effected, and been influenced by, a more sophisticated understanding of the role of transference. Freud and his early followers were aware, of course, of the patient's tendency to "act out"—that is, to actualize transferences with the analyst. Yet, the ways and means of these attempts at actualization, sometimes obvious but more often subtle and elusive, have become better understood as analysts continue to accumulate and compare clinical experiences. Thus, in their discussion of transference, Sandler, Dare, and Holder stress: "It should be added that transference need not be restricted to the illusory apperception of another person . . . but can be taken to include the unconscious (and often subtle) attempts to manipulate or to provoke situations with others which are a concealed repetition of earlier experiences and relationships. It has been pointed out previously that when such transference manipulations or provocations occur in ordinary life, the person towards whom they are directed may either show that he does not accept the role, or may, if he is unconsciously disposed in that direction, in fact accept it, and act accordingly" (1973, p. 48).

This comment on transference indicates—and I believe it reflects a general trend—that analysts have become more attuned to the interactional or interpersonal dimension of transference. A good number of "classical" analysts may still strive toward the ideal of the analyst as "blank screen" or "mirror," but they are nonetheless more aware than their predecessors were of the multiple ways in which the screen/mirror becomes tilted by the analyst's personality and responsivity as these factors enter into the analytic situation. And while vigilance remains the order of the day, there is also a greater curiosity as to just how and why the analyst contributes to the tilt. Moreover, the analyst's emotional reactions, when brought to awareness, are now considered by many "classical" analysts to serve some useful purpose in providing information about patients and their transferences.

This focus on the interactional dimension to transference and countertransference (however defined) is even more pronounced among other analytic schools and investigators. Perhaps most prolific in their exploration of the interactional dimension of the transference and countertransference have been the Sullivanians. Following Sullivan's lead, their focus has been steadily riveted on transference-countertransference, and in their journal, *Contemporary Psychoanalysis*, they have continued to delineate the interpersonal approach. An edited collection of articles from this journal, by Sullivanians and others, appeared under the title *Countertransference* (Epstein and Feiner, 1979), and is to my mind one of the most informative recent works on the subject.

Also contributing to this interactional focus, with a singular perseverance, has been Langs. In the course of about twelve years, he has produced a dozen or so books and founded a journal, *International Journal of Psychoanalytic Psychotherapy*, in which he has systematically outlined the intricacies of an interactional approach, again with the underlying theme that transference and countertransference are mutually, and continuously, interrelated.

Finally, I would include the work of Gill, who in

recent years has parked his ideas on transference and countertransference snugly in the interactional camp. In his important volume, *Analysis of Transference* (1982), and in a number of journal articles, he has elucidated this point of view: "I have suggested a redefinition of transference. The definition would change from the customary one of transference as a distortion of reality defined by the analyst to a conception of a transference-countertransference transaction in which from the differing perspectives of patient and analyst each has a view which has its plausibility" (1983, p. 234).

The means by which patient and therapist influence each other in the transference-countertransference exchange has been delineated in a far more precise and sophisticated fashion than it was in the years of the challenge. The intricate manner in which patient *and* therapist project and introject aspects of each other during the analytic exchange has received much attention, particularly in the work that has been done in the last fifteen years on the complicated interpersonal processes involved in projective identification. Chapter 3 will explore in some detail the concept of projective identification. Suffice it to say here that a rich literature has begun to accumulate on this topic, and it has added considerably to our understanding of the transference-countertransference transaction.

Also adding to our understanding have been the detailed studies of that large group of patients who are neither frankly psychotic nor neurotic: patients with borderline disorders. It is worth noting that the serious early study of these disorders—for example, the seminal papers of Fairbairn and Deutsch in the early 1940s and Knight's work in the early 1950s—began at approximately the same time as the explosion of interest in countertransference.

Patients with borderline pathology tend to evoke intense emotional reactions in their therapists, and thus discussion of technique in these cases inevitably has contributed to a more focused exploration of the nature of countertransference. Likewise, as our conceptual understanding of countertransference has become more sophisticated, it has contributed to more refined technical approaches in the treatment of borderline disorders. Further discussion of these issues will be postponed until Chapter 7, which addresses countertransference in borderline disorders.

In spite of our enhanced understanding of the analyst's responses in the analytic situation, there remains a muddle as to what nomenclature should be given to these responses. There is still no consensus as to what ought to be called *countertransference*. Classical analysts are still inclined to favor a "classical" definition of countertransference, whereby the term is equated with the analyst's transferences to the patient or, more broadly, to other conflict-based responses as well; these responses are generally thought to occur outside of the analyst's awareness.

Two other approaches to the definition of countertransference, both dating from the period of the challenge and both in common usage today, are the totalistic and counterpart views. The *totalistic* approach, first advocated by Heimann, considers *all* of the analyst's responses to the patient as countertransference; these would include both conscious and unconscious responses. The *counterpart* approach defines countertransference as the natural, expectable counter to the patient's transferences or way of interacting. This notion, originally adumbrated by Winnicott in his comments on "objective" countertransference, also includes responses that are experienced consciously or unconsciously by the analyst.

As indicated earlier, I believe that much of the diffi-

culty in arriving at a consensually accepted definition of
the term *countertransference* has been that the linguistic
squabble is enmeshed in a larger controversy over the role
of the analyst in the therapeutic process. Although there
has been some blurring of battle lines since the midcentury, it is still possible to discern some general tendencies.
Thus, I think it correct to say that those analysts espousing a totalistic or counterpart definition of countertransference, in comparison with analysts espousing a
classical definition, are more apt to (1) emphasize the
usefulness of the analyst's emotional responses to the
patient, (2) consider the analyst's qualities as a "real"
person to be of potential value in the curative process
(especially with more disturbed patients), and (3) stress
the value of new experience, and not simply interpretation, as essential to this curative process. I think it is these
important underlying differences in emphasis, and perhaps others as well, which contribute to the controversy
over the definition of countertransference. And until
there is greater agreement on these issues, there will no
doubt remain disagreement over precisely what the term
ought to denote.

   It is with this in mind that I want to mention how I
shall be employing the term *countertransference* in this
book. In my work as a therapist and supervisor, I find that
I use the term somewhat loosely in a totalistic fashion—
that is, to apply to *all* of the therapist's responses to the
patient. But what is of primary interest to me is that type
of response which is the counterpart, or expectable, response to the patient's personality and behavior in the
analytic session. Others have called this *objective countertransference*, and I concur. I distinguish this type of countertransference from the kind of response that is due to
the analyst's personal conflicts or idiosyncrasies—some-

times called *subjective countertransference*. I assume that any of the therapist's responses in the analytic situation will comprise aspects of both objective and subjective countertransference, and it is the therapist's job to tease out and weigh these various aspects. I believe that most analysts today engage in this *process* more or less frequently during their work with the patient, although obviously they do not all accept the terminology I am employing.

Finally, it is worth noting that wide disagreement persists on the question of how, when, and what analysts disclose of their responses to patients. Most analysts, no matter what their orientation, continue to advocate caution regarding the communication of these responses, whether these responses are judged to be of a subjective or objective type. My impression is that *in practice*, analysts do communicate more of their responses than they might theoretically deem advisable. In any case, this book will investigate some of the clinical situations in which self-disclosure would seem to be useful. I believe that this area of technique, left largely unexplored by the pioneering investigators of the challenge period, is one of the major domains of therapeutic technique that requires further exploration.

It might prove informative at this point to elucidate some of these conceptual matters by means of a clinical example. Accordingly, I have selected what is probably the best-known clinical illustration of countertransference (however defined) that we have to date: Freud's response to his patient Irma, as frankly revealed in his famous Dream Specimen of psychoanalysis, "The Irma Injection Dream." Chapter 2, then, is devoted to a brief study of Freud's countertransference(s) as revealed in this dream.

2

Freud's Countertransference

In the summer of 1895, Freud had a momentous dream—
about a patient called Irma. It was a dream that so disturbed and intrigued Freud that for the first time he
submitted a dream of his *own* to systematic interpretation,
freely associating to each element in the dream. As he
finally interpreted it, the meaning of the dream flattered
hardly anyone, least of all Freud himself. Nonetheless, in
the interest of presenting as clearly and cogently as possible his new technique of understanding dreams, Freud
courageously decided to include this dream, along with his
associations, as the introductory clinical specimen in his
magnum opus, *The Interpretation of Dreams*. The dream, as
reported by Freud (1900), is as follows:

A large hall—numerous guests, whom we were receiving.—Among them was Irma. I at once took her
on one side, as though to answer her letter and to
reproach her for not having accepted my "solution"

37

yet. I said to her: "If you still get pains, it's really
only your fault." She replied: "If you only knew
what pains I've got now in my throat and stomach
and abdomen—it's choking me"—I was alarmed and
looked at her. She looked pale and puffy. I thought to
myself that after all I must be missing some organic
trouble. I took her to the window and looked down
her throat, and she showed signs of recalcitrance, like
women with artificial dentures. I thought to myself
that there was really no need for her to do that.—She
then opened her mouth properly and on the right I
found a big white patch; at another place I saw extensive whitish grey scabs upon some remarkable curly
structures which were evidently modelled on the tur-
binal bones of the nose.—I at once called in Dr. M.,
and he repeated the examination and confirmed
it. . . . Dr. M. looked quite different from usual; he
was very pale, he walked with a limp and his chin was
clean-shaven. . . . My friend Otto was now standing
beside her as well, and my friend Leopold was percussing her through her bodice and saying: "She has
a dull area low down on the left." He also indicated
that a portion of the skin on the left shoulder was
infiltrated. (I noticed this, just as he did, in spite of
her dress.) . . . M. said: "There's no doubt it's an
infection, but no matter; dysentery will supervene
and the toxin will be eliminated." . . . We were directly aware, too, of the origin of the infection. Not
long before, when she was feeling unwell, my friend
Otto had given her an injection of a preparation of
propyl, propyls . . . propionic acid . . . trimethylamin (and I saw before me the formula for this
printed in heavy type). . . . Injections of that sort
ought not to be made so thoughtlessly. . . . And probably the syringe had not been clean [p. 107].

Along with this lengthy manifest dream, Freud provided twelve pages of his associations, including a preamble which presented some of the background of the case. It is not possible to do justice here to the elaborate detail in which Freud reported these associations, nor to the intriguing and gripping manner of Freud's presentation (1900, pp. 106–118). Suffice it to say that Freud used his consummate literary skill to draw his reader slowly into what was the mystery of this, his first fully interpreted dream—and, by extension, into the mystery of the Dream itself.

The background of the case immediately, though somewhat mysteriously, established some of the threads of Freud's conflicts. His patient, Irma, was a young widow who happened to be "on very friendly terms" with Freud and his family. Suffering from "hysterical anxiety" and various somatic symptoms, she was being treated by Freud, but only with partial success. Not quite sure how to proceed with the therapy, Freud proposed a "solution" (he does not specify what this was), which the patient rejected. At odds with each other, the treatment was broken off for the summer vacation. On the dream day, Freud had met with Otto, a colleague and friend who in fact had just returned from a resort where he visited with Irma's family. Otto stated to Freud that Irma was "better, but not quite well"—a statement which Freud felt as a reproof. Thus, "in order to justify myself," Freud wrote up the case that evening, with the intention of presenting it to Dr. M., a mutual friend and leading figure in their circle of physicians. With that, Freud went to sleep and dreamt his "Irma Injection Dream."

In his free associations to the dream, Freud took the bold step of allowing the reader to peer into some of the details of his life. Thus, in his associations, Freud made it clear that his patient, Irma, served additionally as a stand-in for a number of women in his life: his wife, his eldest daughter, his governess (when he was a toddler), and another young widow who was a friend of Irma's. Similarly, Dr. M. was a condensation of father figures in Freud's life. In his associations, Freud returned again and again to various of his own wrong-doings—especially in his medical practice—and his longing for exoneration. Less clearly, his associations also meandered back and forth to sexual allusions (e.g., trimethylamin as "one of the products of sexual metabolism"), but here Freud drew the curtain, leaving the reader to form his own conclusions.

The conclusion that Freud articulated regarding the dream's motive and meaning was this:

> The dream fulfilled certain wishes which were started in me by the events of the previous evening (the news given me by Otto and my writing out of the case history). . . . The dream acquitted me of the responsibility for Irma's condition by showing that it was due to other factors—it produced a whole series of reasons. . . . *I* was not to blame for Irma's pains, since she herself was to blame for them by refusing to accept my solution. *I* was not concerned with Irma's pains, since they were of an organic nature and quite incurable by psychological treatment. Irma's pains could be satisfactorily explained by her widowhood (cf. the trimethylamin) which *I* had no means of altering. Irma's pains had been caused by Otto giving her an incautious injection of an unsuitable drug—a thing *I* should never have done. Irma's pains were the result of an injection with a dirty needle, like my old lady's phlebitis—whereas *I* never did any harm with my injections" [1900, pp. 118–119; italics are Freud's].

This explanation of the dream's underlying meaning and motive, as Freud well knew, was only part of the story, although it was enough to render comprehensible the theoretical point he was then intent on making—to wit, that the dream's motive was a fulfillment of the dreamer's wishes. Whatever additional private wishes the dream contained, Freud deliberately, if somewhat provocatively, chose not to articulate. With characteristic candor, though, he acknowledged:

> I will not pretend that I have completely uncovered the meaning of this dream or that its interpretation is without a gap. I could spend more time over it, derive further information from it and discuss fresh problems raised by it. I myself know points from which further trains of thought could be followed. But considerations which arise in the case of every dream of my own restrain me from pursuing my interpretative work. If anyone should feel tempted to express a hasty condemnation of my reticence, I would advise him to make the experiment of being franker than I am [1900, p. 120].

It is perhaps not surprising, in light of the monumental stature of this dream, and of the dreamer, that analysts over the years have probed its content for further meaning. As indicated, Freud himself was aware of other currents in the "Irma Injection Dream," though it is unlikely at the time that he fathomed its full meaning. After all, the dream occurred in 1895—two years before he began his self-analysis and discovered the Oedipus complex, ten years before he formulated his concept of transference, and fifteen years before he enunciated his notion of countertransference. Indeed, it is with the aid of these conceptual tools, provided by Freud and refined by others, that subsequent investigators have been able to mine some of the further meanings of the Dream Specimen of psychoanalysis. It is beyond the scope of this brief chapter to discuss the range of interpretations that other researchers have plumbed from the dream.* What I do wish to accomplish here, in accordance with the focus of this book, is to regard the dream from a single vantage point: Freud's countertransferential dilemma vis-à-vis his patient Irma. In so doing, I hope to highlight some of the important issues regarding the nature of countertransference and, in particular, the technical issue of how the therapist might use countertransference in treatment.

The "Irma Injection Dream," quite obviously, is a particular type of dream: It is the dream of a therapist about his patient, in which the patient appears as herself in the manifest content of the dream. Some recent investigators have referred to this kind of dream as a "countertransference dream" (Whitman et al. 1969, Zwiebel 1985), pointing out that such dreams can be extremely valuable in helping the therapist understand the ongoing transference-countertransference interaction. Zwiebel suggests that this type of dream is likely to occur after the treatment is well underway and, above all, "during an especially problematic or conflict-laden stage of the treatment" (p. 93). He further states that "the countertransference dream should be seen as the sign of a disturbance in the analytic relationship in which both parties take part" (p. 87). Whitman and his associates make the additional point that in the countertransference dream, the patient may be a stand-in for some aspect of the therapist's self. In such a case, part of the disturbance in the ongoing

---

*The reader interested in a thumbnail summary of these investigations is advised to read Elms's excellent contribution (1980).

interaction is that the therapist has become overly identified with the patient—a fact that may be revealed in the
dream by the therapist's fusion of his own body image
with that of the patient.

With these points in mind, then, let me turn to the
Dream Specimen and particularly, Freud's predicament
with Irma. Other researchers have carefully explored the
available biographical materials, compiling what is a rather
detailed knowledge of Freud's personal situation at the
time of the Irma Injection Dream (Elms 1980, Erikson
1954, Hartman 1983). Thus, we know that in July 1895,
Freud was undergoing a period of unusual turmoil in both
his professional and personal life. As Erikson has pointed
out (1954, p. 8), Freud had yet to make his mark profes-
sionally; certainly he had not done so in the way he had
hoped. His private practice was still small and unpredicta-
ble, and his aspirations of gaining academic status were
unfulfilled, partly because he was a Jew and partly because
his theories were unpopular. In fact, so unpopular were
his views as to the sexual etiology of certain nervous
disorders (e.g., hysteria) that Joseph Breuer, his coauthor
of *Studies on Hysteria* (1895), had begun to disengage
himself from Freud. Increasingly, Freud found himself
isolated and rejected by colleagues, despite the fact that he
felt himself ever closer to some momentous discovery.

Freud's professional discontent and turmoil was
echoed in his private life at the time, above all in his
relationship to his wife, Martha (Elms 1980, Hartman
1983, Roazen 1975). Much to her dismay and Freud's as
well, Martha had become pregnant for the sixth time in
nine years, and she was experiencing some ill effects from
this pregnancy. Freud had always been overly concerned
about his wife's health; indeed from the time of their
courtship he had worried that his "ardent embraces" may

be causing her harm (Jones 1953, p. 120, Elms 1980, p. 94). In light of Martha's condition, as well as the prevalent customs, it is likely that Freud was obliged to practice sexual abstinence, or close to it, at the time. Moreover, it is worth noting that precisely as Freud was struggling with all this, his aging father became seriously ill and then died fifteen months later. We now know that within several months of his father's death, Freud undertook his own psychoanalysis, during which he discovered the Oedipus complex.

The turmoil which beset Freud in his professional and personal life found its way into his famous dream. Beneath the layer of interpretation which Freud provided the reader (his concern at having medically damaged Irma) it is now easy to discern some of Freud's underlying sexual concerns and conflicts. Thus, as others have noted (Elms 1980, Erikson 1954, Grinstein 1968, Hartman 1983), Freud's medical examination of Irma has obvious sexual connotations. In the dream, Freud is angry with Irma for not having accepted his "solution" (the German word *losung* has the same double meaning). Freud peers into her mouth, an orifice she opens to him with "recalci-trance," and in it he notes "remarkable curly structures." He notices a portion of her body "in spite of her dress," and he has a friend, Leopold, "percussing her through her bodice." Another friend, Otto, is blamed for having injected Irma with trimethylamin (a sexual byproduct), as Freud thinks to himself in the dream, "Injections of that sort ought not to be made so thoughtlessly. . . . And probably the syringe had not been clean."

Allied to this sexual material is Freud's evident ambivalence and rivalry toward the male figures in the dream. The manifest dream itself, as well as the preamble and several other of Freud's associations, make it clear that

Freud was deeply conflicted in his attitudes toward his male colleagues and friends. He sought to be smarter and better—to outdo them—while at the same time he longed for their approval. This theme is most poignantly represented in the dream by Freud's turning to Dr. M. (who is actually Joseph Breuer) for confirmation of his medical prowess, while at the same time he ridicules and denigrates Dr. M. The latter is rendered "pale," "limp," and "clean-shaven" (i.e., castrated), and his pronouncement that "dysentery will supervene and the toxin will be eliminated," Freud reveals in his associations, is a "ridiculous" statement, and that "I must have been making fun of Dr. M."*

While it is likely that Freud was aware at the time of much of the sexual material in the Dream Specimen (see Hartman 1983, p. 579), it is doubtful whether he then understood the connection between these sexual wishes and his evident rivalry—his Oedipus complex—with the male figures in the dream. Such understanding would come over the next two years, as he coped with the death of his father and turned to self-analysis to work through his oedipal conflict. The Dream Specimen was undoubtedly a step in that direction. It is clear, though, that at the time of this dream, Freud's personal conflicts in this area were not resolved, and were actually exacerbated by the

---

*Recall that, in reality, Freud was at odds with Breuer, his senior colleague and coauthor. Furthermore, Freud believed that Breuer had backed off from the notion of sexual etiology in hysteria in part because he, Breuer, personally could not manage the sexual feelings of these patients; thus, Breuer faltered with his hysteric patient, Anna O. Hence, by publicly analyzing this dream of his struggles with Irma, Freud was asserting that, unlike Breuer, he could grapple with this kind of patient; at the same time, he portrayed his ambivalence by showing that perhaps, like Breuer, he too had failed after all.

current pressures in his life. These conflicts certainly could have interfered with Freud's work with patients. And in the tactfully expressed judgment of several investigators (Elms 1980, Erikson 1954, Grinstein 1968, Hartman 1983), with which I agree, these conflicts did interfere with Freud's treatment of Irma.

These conflicts provided the basis for Freud's "subjective" countertransference. They interfered with Freud's ability to see clearly what was happening inside the patient, as well as what was happening inside himself, and they led him to respond in a nontherapeutic way. But if we are to understand Freud's predicament with Irma, we require more than just an understanding of *his* conflicts. We also need to know what Irma was doing *to him*. We need to know the interactive nature of their relationship—that is, how Irma's conflicts and transference affected Freud's response to her.

Of course, it is quite impossible to ever know this material with any certainty. There are no records of Freud's actual interaction with this patient. Yet in the interest of highlighting the theoretical and technical issue of Freud's countertransference, perhaps I can be permitted to indulge in some speculation. First let me state what we do know about Irma. With the aid of some recent biographical spadework by Hartman (1983), who has built upon the earlier work of others (Anzieu 1959), we now have a clear knowledge of who "Irma" was. Her actual name was Anna Hammerschlag Lichtheim. Her father had been Freud's secondary school teacher of religion, and Freud had maintained a warm relationship with the older man. Anna was the second oldest of four children, and the only daughter. At the time of the dream she was 33 years old. She had been a widow for nine years, her husband having died after they were married only a year. With the

death of her husband, Anna had returned to Vienna—
from Breslau, where she and her husband had been living—and took a small apartment near her parents. Her
father was ailing and she helped care for him. She became
a close friend of Freud's wife, Martha, and socialized with
the Freuds. She also became, according to Jones, a "favorite patient of Freud's" (1953, p. 223).

From Freud's notes and associations to the dream, we
know that Anna/Irma was diagnosed by Freud as a hysteric. She suffered from a variety of symptoms which
Freud believed were neurotically determined: anxiety, feelings of nausea and disgust, stomach pains, and bouts of
choking. In keeping with his new understanding of hysteria, Freud believed that her symptoms were due to repression of her sexual wishes. The "solution" that he proposed to her was most likely an interpretation along these
lines, and he may have implied or openly stated his belief
that her widowhood contributed to her neurosis, and
hence her physical symptoms. Freud would have imparted
this material rather directly, even bluntly. As he so candidly acknowledged: "It was my view at that time (though
I have since recognized it as a wrong one) that my task was
fulfilled when I had informed a patient of the hidden
meaning of his symptoms: I considered that I was not
responsible for whether he accepted the solution or not—
though this is what success depended on" (1900, p. 108).
As we know, Anna did not accept Freud's "solution," and
the treatment at the time of the dream was at an impasse.

One can speculate as to what Anna's role was in
creating this impasse—which today would commonly be
regarded as a transference-countertransference bind. My
principal supposition is this: Just as Freud was struggling
with his unresolved Oedipus complex, so also did his
patient, Anna, suffer from her own Oedipus complex. And

just as Freud's personal circumstances at the time exacerbated his oedipal problem, so in turn did Anna's actual life
situation exacerbate her underlying oedipal problem. It
seems quite likely in these circumstances that Freud—the
admired friend of her father's, the husband of a close
woman friend, and a man with whom she spent several
private hours a week—should come to represent in the
transference her oedipal father.

If this is so, then we can imagine that in her transferential relatedness to Freud she had begun to play out
aspects of her conflict over being the oedipal daughter to
her oedipal father, Freud. Freud would have appeared to
her, probably unconsciously, as both sexually desirable
and dangerously forbidden. Her interaction with him
would therefore have been fraught with hidden sexual
meaning. Indeed, as a hysteric, the very process of talking
to this man and letting herself be known by him would
carry with it on an unconscious level the tantalizing and
dangerous possibility of being *known* in the biblical sense
of that verb, especially if the talk turned to sexual matters.
She would have been torn between the wish to "open up"
to Freud and her fear of letting him know her. It would
not have been at all unusual if she had enacted this
conflict in a manner that was in fact seductive, at one
moment promising to reveal herself, for example, and at
the next moment, in a way that was unwittingly provocative, suddenly becoming "recalcitrant."* She actually
might have done a good deal more, as many hysterics

---

*In an interesting parallel process, Freud's manner of presenting to
the reader some of the more personal details of the dream has a similar
provocative quality. He invites the reader to know him, but then
draws the curtain. He tells the reader that he expects him to be only
briefly interested in his "indiscretions" and then adds in a footnote:

unknowingly do, to create an atmosphere that was subtly seductive, while at the same time fending off awareness of her underlying wishes. But the speculation need not continue here. It is enough to demonstrate that, in Anna's transferential relatedness to Freud, it is likely that some of her behavior was, in reality, covertly seductive. So, up to a point, if Freud felt seduced and then pushed away, there was a reality basis for these countertransferential feelings. In the terminology I am employing, to the extent that Anna actually was relating to Freud in this way, his reaction was an "objective" countertransference.

Freud's technical problem, however, was that he was not at all able to make use of these expectable countertransferential reactions as a way of understanding his patient. He was not able to allow himself to feel like Anna's oedipal father—that is, seduced by his oedipal daughter and then suddenly fended off by her. These feelings were overwhelming to him, and they became entwined with his own subjective problems, such that Anna could no longer be seen for who she was. She became not only Anna, but (on an unconscious level, until the dream) all women who had ever attracted him and yet were inaccessible to him. She was Woman, whom he longed to possess, but dared not possess; Woman, who he wished would accept his "solution," but whom he feared he would contaminate with this solution. In short, Anna became for Freud *his* oedipal mother. And he could not see clearly who she was or what she was doing to him, because

---

"I am obliged to add, however, by way of qualification of what I have said above, that in scarcely any instance have I brought forward the *complete* interpretation of one of my own dreams, as it is known to me. I have probably been wise in not putting too much faith in my reader's discretion" (1900, p. 105; italics are Freud's).

his oedipal conflicts, like hers, were still insufficiently
resolved or understood.*

It is precisely when a therapist is caught in a transference-countertransference bind such as this that he is most
likely to have a "countertransference dream." The dream
is a warning that the therapist is in a morass with the
patient. But, for therapists who have benefited from their
own treatment and learned to work on their own dreams,
the countertransference dream may also serve as a compass. Several investigators have provided candid illustrations of how they were able to use a countertransference
dream to work their way through a transference-countertransference bind (Searles 1965, Tauber 1954, Tower
1956, Zwiebel 1985); in each instance, the therapist used
the dream as a means of evaluating what both he and the
patient were contributing to the current stalemate.

With our current understanding of the value of the
countertransference dream (made possible, of course, by
Freud's original work), we are now able to see how Freud's
dream about Anna could have been useful in the treatment. Principally, it could have been helpful as a source of
information about the hidden meaning of their interaction. In hindsight, it is now possible to imagine that in
their actual interaction, not just in fantasy, both partici-
pants were unknowingly enticing each other, and then
rejecting each other. Anna's part has already been speculated upon. As for Freud, his ongoing relationship with
Anna on both a social and professional basis must have
served as an unconscious allurement to her. Add to this

---

*As revealed in one of Freud's associations, there is a fusion of body
images—Anna's "infiltrated" left shoulder is also Freud's left
shoulder—which, in my view, can be seen as an unconscious recognition on Freud's part of the identical quality of his problems and
Anna's.

Freud's overdetermined need to have her accept his phallic "solution" (interpretations?), and one can easily imagine how *she* may have felt enticed, frightened, and finally rebuffed as Freud faulted her for not "opening up" and accepting his "solution."

To the extent that this is so, the countertransference dream about Anna/Irma could have been used by Freud as a compass in changing therapeutic direction with the patient. The case raises many technical questions, but this discussion will be restricted simply to the issue of how Freud might have usefully employed his countertransference in treating Anna. The question I briefly want to ask, then, is whether, in addition to the "silent" use of countertransference as a source of information about the ongoing interaction, there was also a possibility for "open" use of this countertransference—that is, for disclosure of any of this data to the patient. And if so, what might have been said?

In light of the evident enactment of aspects of the countertransference, I believe that some acknowledgement from the therapist would have had a salutary effect on the patient. This acknowledgement could have been delivered indirectly—in a statement, for example, that the patient was undoubtedly feeling pressured to accept the interpretations. Or, it could have been done somewhat more directly—for example, in a statement that the therapist sensed he was "forcing himself" on the patient, trying to make her "open up," and perhaps also that he realized this was coming from his own needs. The patient's reactions to such disclosure would then be explored. I doubt whether in this case a more specific and direct statement of the countertransference, and specifically the sexualized aspects of the countertransference, would have proved helpful; Anna was frightened enough as it was. In my view, it is also questionable whether it would have been useful, in the manner suggested by Tauber (1954), to selectively disclose fragments of the dream content and invite the patient's associations to this content; again, the patient would probably have only been further enticed and/or frightened. I hasten to add, however, that my aim here is not so much to advocate a specific statement, but more to propose that *some* disclosure could have proved useful and could ultimately have contributed to unravelling the transference-countertransference bind in which Freud and his patient found themselves.

In sum, then, I believe that Freud's countertransference to Anna/Irma, as suggested in his dream, could have been of value in his treatment of her. It could have been used in two ways: (1) silently, as a source of data about the ongoing transference-countertransference interaction, and (2) openly, in a selective disclosure of some of this data to her. Chapters 3 and 4 will explore the theoretical questions involved in this twin usage of countertransference, clarifying further some of the technical issues raised by this most famous example of countertransference, the "Irma Injection Dream."

3

Countertransference as a Source of Information

Although considerable differences in emphasis remain, there is nonetheless widespread agreement today that the analyst's fantasies and feelings toward the patient can provide useful information about the patient. In short, countertransference (whether defined in a totalistic, counterpart, or classical manner) is today widely viewed not simply as a hindrance, but also as a tool of some value in the therapeutic process. This chapter will explore how the analyst's countertransferences can be used as a means of *understanding* the patient and his transferences—that is, the analyst's "silent" use of countertransferential data, as distinguished from open communication of this data (to be discussed in Chapter 4).

I am especially interested in exploring some notions of how the patient may engender countertransference experiences in the analyst—above all, the concepts of projective identification and role-responsiveness. In addition, the concept of "countertransference neurosis" will be examined as it has been employed by Racker, Tower, and others. Finally, the psychology of the analyst will be speculated upon, with particular focus on the personal qualities and early life experiences that seem to predispose the analyst to sensitive awareness of countertransferences.

Early Notions Regarding the Analyst's Responsivity to the Patient

As indicated in Chapter 1, analysts until the midcentury were almost universally cautious—perhaps even "phobic," as Little has suggested—about their emotional responses to their patients. Neutrality was required, even demanded. Yet these early analysts gave freer reign to their more cognitive responses, to their fantasies and associations about their patients and the material they presented. Freud himself encouraged this in his recommendation that the analyst listen to the patient with free-floating attention, which would provide the analyst with a line to the patient's unconscious. Freud described this process as follows:

> To put it in a formula: he [the analyst] must turn his own unconscious like a receptive organ towards the transmitting unconscious of the patient. He must adjust himself to the patient as a telephone receiver is adjusted to the transmitting microphone. Just as the receiver converts back into soundwaves the electric oscillations in the telephone line which were set up by sound waves, so the doctor's unconscious is able, from the derivatives of the unconscious which are communicated to him, to reconstruct that unconscious, which has determined the patient's free associations [1912, pp. 115–116].

In Freud's view, the analyst could rely on his unconscious responsivity to the patient only if the analyst was free of personal conflicts; this freedom was achieved by undergoing personal analysis. Countertransference, as understood by Freud, comprised the conflict-laden reactions that interfered with the analyst's ability, in a sense, to let his mind go—or, in Freud's analogy, to be an accurate, emotionally neutral "telephone receiver." Freud's quasi-scientific but graphic metaphor lacked, of course, a *psychological* explanation of just how the analyst was affected by the patient. This phenomenon was left as something of a mystery; in effect, Freud bequeathed merely the axiom—albeit a fascinating one—that the analyst's unconscious can be exquisitely attuned to that of the patient.

Following Freud, some early researchers sought to provide a psychological explanation for the phenomenon of the analyst's unconscious receptivity to the patient—a phenomenon commonly referred to as the analyst's "intuitiveness." Among the more valuable early writings that touched upon this important capacity in the analyst were those of Deutsch (1926), Reik (1937), and Fliess (1942). In somewhat different terms, all three of these investigators traced the analyst's intuitiveness to his ability to form identifications, primarily on an unconscious level, with the patient's infantile strivings or the objects of these strivings. They pointed out that, while the capacity to form such identifications is essential to the analytic task, there is the inherent danger of the analyst's becoming stuck in these identifications; the analyst then becomes unable to achieve the distance necessary for clarifying and interpreting the patient's transferences. In keeping with the pejorative notion at the time, Reik and Fliess thought of countertransference as that which caused the analyst to get stuck in the identifications. Deutsch, on the other hand, chose to refer to the very formation of these identi-

fications as countertransference—although, as pointed
out earlier, her expanded usage of the term was disre-
garded until some two decades later, when Racker amplified her ideas. These important issues of terminology
notwithstanding, what Deutsch, Reik, and Fliess all
accomplished was to provide an initial basis for explaining
what went on inside the analyst, and how these experiences were useful in understanding the patient. Yet they
left largely undeveloped the other side of the interpersonal
equation—that is, how the patient managed to "get to"
the analyst and engender his responses.

Projective Identification and Countertransference

In the late 1940s and early 1950s—the "challenge" period, as I have called it—there was a sudden burst of
interest in countertransference issues among many sec-
tors of the psychoanalytic community. In some of the
papers published during that period, analysts began to
recount with great candor just what it was that occurred
inside themselves during the psychoanalytic process, and
they began to seek more precise explanations as to how the
patient influenced or engendered these reactions. To reiterate two points made in Chapter 1, there was an increas-
ing recognition that (1) all of the analyst's reactions, including some emotional reactions, could be of use in
understanding the patient, and (2) the patient's transferences and the analyst's countertransferences are linked in
an ongoing and reverberating manner.

It was in the fertile soil of this period that the concept
of *projective identification* took root. The concept of projective identification was used to explain how some patients

evoke, by their transferences, corresponding, intense countertransferences in their therapists. In other words, projective identification addressed the objective component of the countertransference. It explained how various disturbing countertransferences—hopelessness, fear, boredom, envy, giddiness, and sexual responses of all kinds—could have a source in the patient's transferences. Projective identification went to the heart of the patient–therapist interaction. Yet, as a product of Klein's distinctive garden, it was also an idea that at times became entangled in the controversy between Kleinians and other analysts.

In this section, I will outline the development of the concept of projective identification, from its introduction by Klein in 1946 to some of its usages by more recent proponents. In so doing, I will also discuss some of the controversial and ill-defined aspects of the concept. I expect it will be clear, however, that I consider projective identification to be of enormous value in explaining a variety of countertransference experiences and, in particular, how these experiences are engendered by the patient.

Klein introduced the concept of projective identification in "Notes on Some Schizoid Mechanisms" (1946); she later amplified it in "On Identification" (1955). As outlined by Klein, projective identification comprises a process or method by which the infant relates to external objects during the first three months of life—the "paranoid-schizoid" phase of development, as she called this period. Projective identification involves the use of the mechanisms of splitting, projection, and identification in the following manner. First, the infant employs the defense mechanism of *splitting* in an ongoing effort to keep his "good internal objects" (the loving parts of the self) separate and safe from the "bad internal objects" (the aggression-filled parts of self). The infant further fanta-

sizes expelling—or *projecting*—either the split-off good
internal objects or the split-off bad internal objects
(though usually the bad ones) and lodging these objects in
another person, typically the mother. Finally, the infant
feels intimately bound up with—that is, *identified* with—
the recipient of these projections: hence, the term *projective identification.*

Klein pointed out that this process, characteristic of
infants at the earliest phase of development, is also common in adults who are fixated at, or have temporarily
regressed to, this phase. She makes it clear that, for all
who engage in projective identification, there is a heavy
price to pay. The individual who fantasizes that his bad
internal objects are expelled and lodged in another then
feels persecuted by the other. And when the good internal
objects have been projected onto the other, the recipient
becomes overly idealized as the source of all goodness. In
either case, the individual who is engaged in projective
identification feels caught up with the other in a tie that
binds. His reduced or impoverished self needs to remain in
contact with, and in control of, the recipient of those split-
off parts of himself. To lose contact with and control over
the other is experienced as losing contact with and control
over part(s) of the self. In some of her later writings,
Klein offered examples demonstrating the patient's use of
projective identification. She did not take the additional
step of exploring how the projective identifications were
received by the therapist and, specifically, how they might
engender the therapist's countertransferences.

It was not long, however, before some of Klein's
followers and admirers did take this step. Employing examples from their clinical work, these investigators made
explicit—as Klein had not—how the patient uses projective identification to *actually* engender in the therapist the

experience of the split-off and unwanted parts of the patient's self. They demonstrated how projective identification involved not only a fantasy on the patient's part, but also an attempt, subtle or blatant, to manipulate the therapist's internal experience. Rosenfeld (1952, 1954) and Bion (1955) showed how projective identification is employed in an aggressive, and sometimes violent, manner by patients who are psychotic or have severe character disorders. They also made clear that by monitoring the induced countertransferences, the therapist is able to understand the patient's internal experience. As Bion asserted, "for a considerable proportion of the analytic time the only evidence on which an interpretation can be based is that which is afforded by the countertransference" (1955, p. 224).

In one poignant example, Bion described how a schizoid patient had managed by means of a projective identification to induce a frightening countertransference experience. Bion discussed how he used this experience to help the patient.

The patient had been lying on the couch, silent, for some twenty minutes. During this time I had become aware of a growing sense of anxiety and tension which I associated with facts about the patient which were already known to me from work done with him in the six months he had already been with me. As the silence continued I became aware of a fear that the patient was meditating a physical attack on me, though I could see no outward change in his posture. As the tension grew I felt increasingly sure that this was so. Then, and only then, I said to him, "You have been pushing into my insides your fear that you will murder me." There was no change in the patient's position but I noticed that he clenched his fists till the skin over the knuckles became white. The silence was unbroken. At the same time I felt that the tension in the room, presumably in the relationship between him and me, had decreased. I said to him, "When I spoke to you, you took your fear that you would murder me back into yourself; you are now feeling afraid you will make a murderous attack upon me." I followed the same method throughout the session, waiting for impressions to pile up until I felt I was in a position to make my interpretation [1955, p. 224].

For Bion, the process by which the therapist "contains" the split-off and unwanted parts of the patient and then returns them in the form of an interpretation (thus implying that the therapist is not overwhelmed by the projection) is, in essence, the curative factor in psychoanalytic treatment. In some of his later work (1963, 1965, 1970), Bion further underscored the significance of the analyst's function as a "container" of the patient's projections, though, as shall be discussed next, Bion's reprojection of the contained material in the form of rather quick, deep interpretations is a technical matter open to debate.

Other followers of Klein further applied the concept of projective identification to explain the behavior of neurotics. Money-Kyrle (1956) and Racker (1953, 1957) both provided lucid examples from their clinical work with these healthier patients. Racker, in particular, made an almost encyclopedic effort to categorize the various types of induced countertransferences that issue from corresponding projections on the part of the patient. The work of Racker and Money-Kyrle (and also Heimann, although she did not specifically use the term *projective identifica-*

tion in her landmark paper in 1950) suggested that use of this primitive mechanism was by no means restricted to more severely disturbed patients. Rather, projective identification was employed at times by all people in the course of human interaction.

This was a controversial point, for, if projective identification involves a blurring of boundaries between projector and recipient, then in what manner do healthier individuals—for whom self and object boundaries are differentiated—employ this mechanism? The obvious answer, implied in these early papers, was that everyone experiences an occasional blurring of boundaries between self and others. This argument, which received more explicit attention in the work of later investigators, will be taken up later.

The elaboration of the concept of projective identification and its effect on countertransference has been continued in the last twenty years or so by a number of investigators, many of whom are non-Kleinians. For instance, Searles, in some of his papers on the treatment of borderline and schizophrenic patients (1965, 1979), has provided a dramatic and lively sense of what it is like to be the recipient and container of the patient's projective identifications. Like Bion, Searles uses the induced feelings as a barometer to gauge what is happening inside the patient. Searles asserts even more explicitly than did Bion that the therapist, in remaining open to the patient's projections, is apt to become transiently quite disturbed at various times during the treatment. Searles argues that it is precisely the therapist's willingness to enter into a deep participation with the patient that enables him to understand the patient. The therapist must not become inextricably overwhelmed by his countertransferential experience of the patient's projective identification; rather, he must process it and integrate it into his own healthier personality. Then, by means of an emotionally modulated statement or interpretation about the interaction (and unlike Bion, Searles selectively discloses his countertransferences), the therapist can make the modified and integrated projection available for reinternalization by the patient.

This process, as outlined by Searles, has been discussed by other writers, also from a non-Kleinian perspective. Ogden (1979), following the earlier work of Malin and Grotstein (1966), has suggested that we expand the definition of projective identification to include the entire process whereby an individual (1) projects or expels an unwanted part of the self, (2) desposits this part in another person, and (3) recovers a modified version of what was extruded. This is an extension of Klein's notion, in which "recovery" plays no role. Moreover, while Klein focused on the patient's *fantasy* of how his projection affected the recipient, Ogden's principal emphasis, much like Searles's, is on the *actual* manner in which the recipient manages and handles the projection. As outlined by Ogden, constructive management of the projection involves the recipient's willingness to absorb and accept the induced countertransferential feelings and to use these feelings as a basis for understanding the patient. Like other investigators, including Winnicott, Ogden compares the therapist's constructive management of the patient's projections to the therapeutic manner in which mothers manage their children's projections.

In an interesting hypothetical illustration, Ogden writes:

> Let us imagine that a child is frightened by his wish to destroy and annihilate anyone who frustrates or opposes him. One way of his handling these feelings

would be to project unconsciously his destructive wishes in fantasy into his mother, and through the real interaction with her, engender [these] feelings . . . e.g., by making a major battle out of his eating, his toileting, his dressing, getting him to sleep at night and up in the morning, leaving him with another caretaker, etc. The mother might unrealistically begin to feel that she perpetually storms around the house in a frenzy of frustrated rage ready to kill those that stand between her and what she desires. . . . On the other hand, "good enough" handling of the projected feelings might involve the mother's ability to integrate the engendered feelings with other aspects of herself, e.g., her healthy self-interest, her acceptance of her right to her anger and resentment at her child for standing in the way of what she wants, her confidence that she can contain such feelings without acting on them with excessive withdrawal or retaliatory attack. . . . Through the mother's interactions with the child, the processed projection (which involves the sense of the mother's mastery of her frustrated feelings and destructive, retaliatory wishes) would be available to the child for re-internalization [1979, p. 364].

Langs (1975, 1976b, 1979, 1980), another non-Kleinian, has carefully delineated the manifold ways in which the therapist may fail to master the feelings induced by the patient's projective identifications. Langs argues, as did some early Kleinians, that projective identification is a "universal mechanism and is used by individuals at every level of functioning" (1976b, p. 150). In the treatment situation, the therapist's principal task is to contain and metabolize the patient's projective identifications. The induced feelings and fantasies are used as a source of information and insight about the patient. In Langs's view, therapists all too frequently fail in this task, and instead reproject the nonmetabolized material back onto the patient, who then typically becomes even more anxious, sensing that his projections are indeed menacing. To add further injury, Langs asserts, therapists quite often reproject not only the patient's original projections, but also elements of their own pathological selves.

Thus, for example, a patient may attempt to project onto the therapist an unwanted homosexual part of himself about which he is feeling somewhat anxious. The therapist, unable to contain and metabolize the induced feelings and fantasies because of his own even more extreme homosexual fears, reprojects this material along with his own pathological accretions. The therapist might do this by offering a premature and exaggerated interpretation to the patient—suggesting, perhaps, that the patient feels he will go crazy and may become suicidal if he were to have homosexual feelings. Langs is convinced that this type of pathological interaction is quite common in the "bi-personal field," and he characterizes much of the work of his colleagues as "lie therapy." My view is that Langs presents a valuable perspective, even if at times he may go so far as to induce in his own "bi-personal field" (among supervisees and readers, for example) some troubling feelings of worthlessness and corrosive guilt.

Finally, I would like to mention the work of Kernberg (1975, 1984), who also has added to the literature on projective identification. Kernberg maintains that projective identification is a primitive form of projection. In projective identification, the subject maintains a sense of "empathy" with what is projected and a wish to interact with and control the object of the projective identification; in projection, on the other hand, there is a lack of empathy with what is projected and a distancing or sense of estrangement from the object. In Kernberg's view, projection is typically used by neurotics, and projective identification by borderlines and psychotics. Kernberg (1975) has made a rich contribution to the understanding of how borderline patients employ projective identification, and has provided a vivid characterization of the induced countertransferential feelings that often arise within the therapist. In a manner that suggests his Kleinian roots, Kernberg tends to translate these induced feelings into rather quick and deep interpretations—above all, interpretations of the patient's aggressive feelings and fantasies. This technique, as I have stated, is open to debate.

At this point, I want to discuss what I believe are some of the ill-defined and controversial aspects of the concept of projective identification and its influence on countertransference. By now the concept of projective identification has received widespread attention and is no longer the product of any one school of psychoanalytic thought. As Ogden has persuasively argued: "The concept of projective identification is entirely separable from a Kleinian theoretical or developmental framework. . . . In particular, there is no necessary tie between projective identification and the death instinct, the concept of envy, the concept of constitutional aggression, or any other facet of specifically Kleinian clinical theory or metapsychology" (1979, p. 364).

Although the concept of projective identification has become more widely accepted, the usage of the term has remained imprecise. There is still some difference of opinion and emphasis over the question of *who* uses projective identification—healthier individuals as well as more disturbed people? There is broad agreement that the mechanism is frequently employed by borderline and psychotic patients. But not everyone would agree with the view of some analysts (Money-Kyrle and Langs, for example) that projective identification is commonly used by neurotic patients as well. I fundamentally accept this point of view, however, and, in agreement with these investigators, would contend that the clear-edged differentiation between self and others may give way to a temporary blurring of boundaries in situations of deep interpersonal contact, such as occur in the patient–therapist interaction, or for that matter, in the intimacy of husband–wife and parent–child relationships. I believe this to happen rather commonly even among neurotic and normal people, although less commonly than among more disturbed individuals. One need not—and with healthier individuals, one seldom does—lose an *overall* sense of differentiation between oneself and the other. The blurring takes place in the *one sector* of the self that is engaged in the interaction.

I would now like to consider some issues regarding the therapist's reception of the patient's projective identifications. One problematic area concerns the manner and extent to which the patient's extruded part can be said to replicate itself in the therapist's experience. Is there a truly "objective" countertransference? Or is the therapist bound to alloy the received projection with aspects of his own personality?

Consider an example: If a narcissistic patient attempts to expel and deposit in the therapist his unwanted, devalued self (including his feelings of worthlessness and humiliated defeat), does the therapist experience himself as devalued in the same manner as the patient in his unconscious experience? Obviously there is no way of knowing for sure. Critics of the concept of projective identification point out that the notion of "putting parts of oneself into another" would seem to imply that the object is an empty container. And, indeed, advocates of the concept do sometimes provide clinical examples in which it is implied that an exact replication of the patient's experience in the therapist does take place. However, a number of more careful expositors of the concept (Kernberg, Langs, and Ogden, for example) stress that the induced experiences are apt to be colored more or less by the therapist's own personality and particular level of organization. The therapist's knowledge of his own "personal equation," largely gleaned from personal analysis, enables him to better evaluate the manner and degree to which he may have colored the patient's projection with his own subjective elements. The therapist can then hope to come up with a good approximation, a hard-won and sophisticated hunch, about the patient's inner experience. This hunch, in the context of everything else the therapist knows about the patient, is of value in the therapeutic work. In sum, the concept of projective identification, if applied with a sense of caution and humility, can be of use in understanding the patient.

As a further and related observation, I would like to emphasize that for patients engaged in a projective identification, the "understanding" they seek in the therapist is not simply a cognitive knowing, but an *emotionally involved* knowing. Patients must sense that they are, in some measure, "getting to" the therapist. Otherwise, they will feel that they have made no contact, established no communication. They need the therapist to take in the split-off, unwanted part and make it part of the therapist's self, and they need the therapist to do this without becoming overwhelmed by it. They want the therapist to consume it, without being consumed by it. And they look for cues that this is happening.

The therapist can provide these cues by talking—offering clarifications and interpretations—or by remaining silent. In reading the literature on the management of

projective identifications, one is struck by the vast differences in therapeutic procedures that are deemed appropriate. Bion seems to offer deep, quick interpretations of
the patient's material in a dry, unflinching tone; Searles
interprets the patient's material in a less detached manner
and talks about his own feelings and fantasies; Langs
seems to prefer more silence; and so on. All these approaches and styles are viable *in principle*, even though
some patients (not diagnostic categories) might fit better
with one approach than another. Each approach has its
own drawbacks: Silence can feel to a given patient more
like *with*holding than holding; an interpretation, especially a quick and deep one, can be experienced not as a
digested or metabolized offering, but as a regurgitation or
reprojection. What is crucial is the patient's registering of
the therapist's response, and the therapist's sensitivity to
the patient's act of registering. I am aware that what I am
saying here is evident to many therapists. In discussions
of technique, however, advocacy of a particular approach
(the one that works for oneself), and disparagement of
another, is too often the order of the day. I say all this as a
necessary addendum to the position taken in this book—
namely, that the therapist's disclosure of countertransferential feelings is, in *my* experience, at times a useful way
of providing the patient with a sense of being "understood."

Role-Responsiveness and Countertransference

An interesting and valuable alternate explanation of how
the therapist uses countertransferences to understand the
patient has been provided by Sandler in his seminal article

"Countertransference and Role-Responsiveness." Sandler (1976) eschews the concept of projective identification as simply insufficient "to explain the processes of dynamic interaction which occur in the transference and counter-transference" (p. 47). He seems to believe that the notion of projective identification suggests too one-sided a view, paying insufficient attention to the multiple cues given and received by *both* patient *and* therapist during their exchanges with each other. He believes that the concept of *role-responsiveness* more adequately addresses the interactive and interpenetrating nature of the patient–therapist relationship.

Essential to Sandler's concept of role-responsiveness is his view that the patient's transference represents not simply a static illusion about the therapist; rather, it also involves "an attempt by him to impose an interaction, an interrelationship (in the broadest sense of the word) between himself and the analyst" (p. 44). The patient attempts to *manipulate* the analyst into playing out a specific role. The manner and extent to which the analyst experiences and plays out this role will depend on his own personal tendencies. The analyst's actual response— overt, as well as in his thoughts and feelings—can be regarded as "a compromise formation between his own tendencies and *his reflexive acceptance of the role which the patient is forcing on him*" (p. 46; italics are Sandler's). In the terminology I am using, the analyst's reflexive role-response would be an *objective countertransference*, and his own tendencies would be *subjective countertransference*, with aspects of both contributing to the analyst's actual response.

Sandler provides case illustrations from his own analytic work, candidly describing how he has found himself enacting particular roles which, in large measure, were choreographed for him by the patient. In one example, Sandler discusses how in the early phase of treatment with one young man, he found himself talking excessively during sessions, unwittingly picking up the slack whenever there was a pause in the conversation. Sandler found himself worrying that any silence at all would cause the young man to abruptly terminate treatment. Upon closer examination, he noted how the patient, by a slight inflection of his voice, managed to end every sentence with an interrogation, although he seldom formulated a direct question. Sandler finally pointed out this pattern to the patient, who promptly recalled how as a boy he had compulsively engaged his father in conversation when he came home from work. He was wounded by his father's inattentiveness and emotional withdrawal, and he had always longed for the father's engaged involvement with him. Accordingly in the treatment, Sandler suggests, the patient subtly attempted to get the analyst to play out the role of a responsive and involved father, and Sandler, in his own way, had begun to enact this role. It might also be noted (though Sandler seems less focused on this aspect) that Sandler was also manipulated into enacting and experiencing the role of the worried and insecure boy who might be abandoned at any moment by the father (patient).

The case material presented by Sandler could also be conceptualized in terms of projective identification. Quite simply, one can speak of both the patient's attempt to project and lodge in the analyst the frightened, worried part of himself that feared abandonment by the father and the patient's attempt to project and lodge in the analyst the introject of ideal, attentive father. As long as one keeps in mind that projective identification is not merely a fantasy, but in addition involves an actual attempt to manipulate the other person in the interaction, it would seem that this way of conceptualizing the data is also viable and useful.

Sandler's notion of role-responsiveness does, however, have the benefit of bringing into sharp focus the interactive nature of the patient–therapist exchange. It underscores that the therapist is an *active* participant in assuming the role. The notion of projective identification, as employed by some of its early proponents—not least of all, Klein—would seem to suggest a more *passive* recipient (therapist). Yet I believe that some of the more recent work on projective identification (Ogden 1979 and, above all, Langs 1976b) does sufficiently take into account the therapist's activity in cuing the patient that he is open to receive a given projection and, subsequently, that he has processed the projection.

A further benefit of the interactional emphasis in Sandler's approach is that it makes evident that at the same time as the patient casts the therapist in a given role, he casts himself in a "complementary" role. Thus, for example, while the therapist is cast in the role of an ideal, attentive father, the patient is a frightened, needy boy. This point of view can also be found in some of the work on projective identification—perhaps most notably in Racker's work. But quite often it is either left as an implicit assumption, as in some of Ogden's examples, or not noted at all.

In sum, Sandler's notion of role-responsiveness is a valuable alternate way of looking at the relationship between some of the therapist's countertransferences and the patient's transferences, and at how the former may be useful in providing information about the latter. I do not think, however, that the concept of role responsiveness supplants the concept of projective identification. Both would seem to address the same clinical material in potentially insightful, if somewhat differently focused, ways.

The Countertransference Neurosis

The concepts of role-responsiveness and projective identification both point to the analyst's reactivity to the patient's transferential wishes and aims. Proponents of both
concepts advocate that the therapist must leave himself
open to experiencing the impact of these transference
maneuvers. The therapist's receptivity is a two-edged
sword, however. On the one hand, the therapist can use
his countertransferential experiences to understand the
patient. On the other, he can become overwhelmed by
these experiences and inextricably entangled in a transference-countertransference bind, to the detriment of both
the patient and himself.

As proposed by Racker (1953), the notion of countertransference neurosis was an effort to address this dilemma. Racker was proposing his notion at a time when
analysts were just beginning to consider that countertransference might be of some value in the analytic work,
and not merely a hindrance. In a manner that was provocative and even polemical, Racker suggested that every
transference neurosis in the patient tended to produce a
corresponding countertransference neurosis in the analyst. The precise form of this countertransference neurosis, the degree of intensity, and the consciousness of it
could be expected to differ from analyst to analyst; each
analyst, after all, brought to the psychoanalytic situation
his own characteristic features, his own "personal equation." The therapist's task was to neither resist the countertransference neurosis nor to "drown" in it, as Racker
phrased it. By "splitting" his own ego such that one part
participates and the other observes, the analyst could hope
to gain a valuable emotional understanding of the patient's
inner world.

Racker employed the term *countertransference neurosis* to designate a gamut of potential responses from the analyst, ranging from short-lived, internal experiences to relatively intense and prolonged experiences that are acted out by the analyst. His conclusion was that the countertransference neurosis could be destructive when enacted with the patient. But if the analyst were able to experience it internally without playing it out, his neurosis could be of immense value in understanding the patient. This was a controversial conclusion at that time, and it was made all the more controversial by Racker's choice of the phrase *countertransference neurosis*. Today, Racker's conclusions are far more widely accepted, and while few analysts have adopted Racker's phrase, there are a number who argue that the analyst's useful countertransferential response might involve a more intense and active involvement with the patient than even Racker had deemed advisable.

One early analyst who assumed this more radical position was Tower, a contemporary of Racker's. While somewhat hesitant to accept the term *countertransference neurosis*, she nonetheless argued that, as part of the curative process, the analyst might need to become intensely involved and caught up in his countertransference to the patient. As she put it, "I doubt that there is any thorough working through of a deep transference neurosis, in the strictest sense, which does not involve some form of emotional upheaval in which *both* patient and analyst are involved" (1956, pp. 249–250; italics are Tower's). Tower asserted that the analyst's countertransference neurosis often involves an actual playing out or enactment with the patient. She provided frank case material of her own to demonstrate the potential usefulness of this type of countertransferential involvement. Tower believed that the analyst's becoming caught up in the countertransference enables him to "emotionally understand" the patient. Even more radical was her implication that the patient needs to sense that he has so engaged the therapist. Having become engaged in this transference-countertransference bind, both therapist and patient then struggle to work their way out of the entanglement. What evolves is a new experience that amounts to a healthier, less neurotic way of relating to each other.

This radical notion of the utility of the analyst's countertransference neurosis can be found in the work of a number of contemporary investigators (Bollas 1983, Levenson 1972, Searles 1979, Spotnitz 1976). These writers generally do not employ the phrase *countertransference neurosis*, but they all assume that the analyst often becomes transiently ill as part of the curative process with a given patient. While this is more emphatically stated for the treatment of psychotic or borderline patients, it is also considered to play a part in the treatment of less disturbed patients. Bollas puts this position as follows: "We know that the analytic space and process facilitates regressive elements in analyst as well as in patient, so each analyst working with, rather than against, the countertransference must be prepared, on occasion, to become rather *situationally ill,* in so far as his receptivity to the reliving of the patient's transference will inevitably mean that the patient's representation of disturbed bits of the mother, or the father, or elements of the infant self, will be utilized in the transference usage of the analyst" (1983, pp. 5–6; italics are Bollas's).

I believe it is precisely in this sense of the analyst's countertransferential involvement with the patient that the phrase *countertransference neurosis* retains a certain usefulness. I do not believe that the phrase ought to apply to relatively mild, short-lived countertransference experiences; these experiences, even when predominantly of an idiosyncratic or "subjective" nature, do not amount to an illness or neurosis in the therapist. As I see it, the phrase would seem to make sense in designating a more intense and prolonged countertransferential involvement, in which one's feelings are profoundly affected and one finds oneself unable to stand back and take full stock of what is happening. One is unable to be "oneself." In such situations, the therapist may inadvertently enact the countertransference in small, or not so small, ways.

It is when the analyst finds himself in this predicament that he is often in a position to be most therapeutic or most destructive to the patient. In agreement with Tower and others, I note that when I look back at the cases in which the most meaningful therapeutic results were achieved, this kind of deep and precarious involvement often occurred. The involvement was precarious for the reason that, had I not worked through the countertransference neurosis, the experience surely would have been unhelpful, and probably destructive, to the patient. The advantage of entering the gravitational force of the patient's transference and experiencing a countertransference neurosis is that one is then in a position of understanding from *within*. The patient senses when this has happened. Again in agreement with Tower, I believe it is in the process of working one's way back out of this entanglement along with the patient that the psychoanalytic method can have its sharpest cutting edge. Transference interpretations have great impact because they are made in this living context of a "new experience" between patient and therapist.

This kind of patient–therapist experience can occur in the psychoanalytic treatment of *all* patients. In general, borderline and psychotic patients engage the therapist in a countertransference neurosis of greater intensity and *sturm und drang*. But perhaps even more important in determining the profundity of this development is the particular match-up of a given therapist and a given patient, no matter what the diagnosis of either. The point is simply that such a development is of great potential value. And just as the patient's transference neurosis plays a crucial role in the psychoanalytic process, so can the countertransference neurosis, in the manner I am describing, also serve a vital function.

The Therapist's Capacity to Use Countertransferences

I think it accurate to say that some therapists are more gifted than others with a capacity to be sensitively aware of their countertransference experiences. This is so just as it is so that some therapists demonstrate a greater capacity for comprehending and making use of dreams, or body and postural cues, or the results of psychodiagnostic tests. To be sure, one's formal education and training (including one's personal analysis) and experience with patients contribute to the development of these capacities. But special talent or potential ability in any of these areas would seem to be rooted in the personality and character structure of the therapist—ultimately traceable to innate gifts and early life experiences.

In this section, I will offer some speculations on those personal qualities and early life experiences that would seem to predispose the therapist to a sensitive awareness of his countertransferences. This is rather murky terrain, and I do not pretend to have explored it thoroughly, but I do want to talk about where I have arrived so far.

When a therapist is employing his countertransference to gain an emotional understanding of a patient, he essentially does two things: (1) He allows himself—in his internal experience—to participate emotionally in the drama directed by the patient, and (2) he stands back and observes his own participation with the patient. The ability to enter into this drama, to participate in a role or identity as prescribed by the patient, requires of the therapist a capacity to be influenced by another. Actually, it requires more: It demands a certain taste for this kind of influence from another, a rather unusual readiness to be used emotionally by another. The ability to stand back and observe one's participation, however, calls upon an opposite tendency in the therapist—namely, a disposition to withdraw from this kind of influence and an unwillingness to be impinged upon by the other.

The following question then arises: What kind of personal qualities and early life experiences might be conducive to the development of these capacities and, moreover, this specific ambitendency in the therapist? We can find at least a partial answer to this question by focusing on a particular type of child (who later becomes a therapist) and a particular type of early life situation in which this child grows up psychologically.

The kind of child I have in mind is one whose gifts include a kind of intelligence and sensitivity that enables him to be emotionally responsive to others. Such a child often, from very early in life, strikes others as hypersensitive to stimuli—a child whose "telephone receiver," to use Freud's phrase, is unusually tuned in. What happens to this child is that his unusual sensitivity is noticed and needed by one or another of his parents, usually the mother. The parent, for reasons both characterological and circumstantial, comes to lean emotionally on this child in ways that are often excessive, yet subtle. The child becomes the parent's "ear" and, long after it might have been in the child's best interests to tune out this parent, the child remains enmeshed in this role. To use the language of other investigators who have also discussed the psychology of the therapist, we may say that the child is used by the parent as a selfobject (Kohut 1971) or as a narcissistic extension of the parent (Miller 1979). Miller summarizes this phenomenon as follows: "It is often said that psycho-analysts suffer from a narcissistic disturbance. . . . His [the analyst's] sensibility, his empathy, his intense and differentiated emotional responsiveness, and his unusually powerful 'antennae' seem to predestine him as a child to be used—if not misused—by people with intense narcissistic needs" (p. 54).

To be used as a selfobject or narcissistic extension of a parent has both benefits and costs. The child senses his specialness and at an early age often experiences himself as older and wiser than others, including the other members of his family and his peers. The child feels himself to be, in a word, important. The price paid for this sense of specialness is that the child remains tied to this parent, unable to separate emotionally from him or her. I am not talking about physical separation, of course; such a child often has an air of excessive independence and maturity about him. I am talking, rather, about the child's being emotionally yoked to the parent, his own identity submerged in that of the parent to the point—as Miller suggests, employing Winnicott's terminology—that the child's "true self" remains underdeveloped. And therein arises a dilemma. To feel special, important, and most intensely alive and related, the child must be in this kind of relationship with another person—the parent or some replacement for the parent. Yet to be in such a relationship is also to feel, concurrently or alternatingly, a loss of one's sense of self and an uncomfortable sensation of being taken over by the other.

It is this dilemma and corresponding ambitendency that the child brings to his subsequent life experiences, and if he should happen to become a therapist, he brings this along with him. With good training, and most especially, a good analytic experience, he can learn to recognize his special vulnerability—and gift—and he can learn to establish and feel alive in relationships in which being merged and submerged play a far lesser part. But, I submit, a certain ambivalent longing remains for this primordial type of relationship, and in the regressive pull of psychoanalytic treatment, this longing is again set into motion. However, the therapist working with his patient is now in a more protected situation than he once was as a child with his parent. He has the benefit of his personal analysis, the formal structure of the treatment situation (time-limited sessions, no social contacts, and so on), and the availability of colleageal supervision to shield him from becoming entrapped in this primordial relationship. Besides, if all else fails, he can acknowledge failure and let the patient go.

Thus protected, the therapist can now enter into this relationship with the patient and let himself be induced or seduced into any particular role that the patient desires. He can allow himself once again to be used emotionally by a person in need, and once again he can feel his importance to this person and savor that special sense of intense liveliness that comes with such an involvement. But then he must step back, for the patient's sake *and* his own sake. He cannot afford to "drown" in the experience as he once (almost) did as a child. Here he is helped not only by his training and his professionalism, but also by his own character structure and, in particular, that side of his ambivalence which does *not* wish to be impinged upon and taken over by the other. And so he steps back, becomes "himself" again, and observes how he has participated in the patient's drama. His emotional participation with the patient then becomes a tool in the service of the treatment. The therapist's gift—and vulnerability—which probably did not "cure" the parent (Searles 1975), can at last be put to full use. Otherwise stated, he is able to be reparative to his patient in a way that he was not able to be reparative to his parent.

It is this process that the therapist is drawn to again and again: merging with and separating from the patient, participating with him and then standing back and observing his participation. It is my hypothesis that the kind of therapist who is most gifted in using his countertransference is apt to be a person who is able—and in fact predisposed—to engage in this merging–separating process. I have outlined some of the personal qualities and early life experiences that are likely to contribute to such a predisposition. I am aware that this is only one possible explanation for the development of a facility in using countertransferential data. It is, however, an explanation that seems to fit for a number of therapists who have impressed me as possessing talent in this area.

4

The Disclosure of Countertransference

In reality, however, it may happen that we can only with difficulty tolerate certain external or internal features of the patient, or perhaps we feel unpleasantly disturbed in some professional or personal affair by the analytic session. Here, too, I cannot see any other way out than to make the source of the disturbance in us fully conscious and to discuss it with the patient, admitting it perhaps not only as a possibility but as a fact [Ferenczi 1933, p. 159].

A patient of mine, a very bad obsessional, was almost loathsome to me for some years. I felt bad about this until the analysis turned a corner and the patient became lovable, and then I realized that his unlikeableness had been an active symptom, unconsciously determined. It was indeed a wonderful day for me (much later on) when I could actually tell the patient that I and his friends had felt repelled by him, but

that he had been too ill for us to let him know. This
was also an important day for him, a tremendous
advance in his adjustment to reality [Winnicott 1949,
p. 70].

Analysts often behave unconsciously exactly like the
parents who put up a smoke screen, and tantalize their
children, tempting them to see the very things they
forbid their seeing; and not to refer to counter-transference is tantamount to denying its existence, or
forbidding the patient to know or speak about it
[Little 1951, p. 38].

These three quotations all touch upon one of the
more controversial areas of psychoanalytic technique: the
therapist's open communication of his countertransference experiences. The point of view represented by these
three early mavericks still arouses considerable suspicion
among analysts. I think it accurate to say that while most
analysts today do find value in the "silent" use of countertransferential data (as a source of information about the
patient), the majority remain chary of, or outright opposed to, disclosing this data to the patient. There is,
however, a growing minority who, in the tradition of
Ferenczi, Winnicott, and Little, have experimented with
the selective disclosure of countertransference, and who
have found that such disclosures can be, on occasion, of
vast therapeutic value. I agree with this minority. Accordingly, the main thrust of this chapter will be to outline this
point of view. To be discussed are such issues as what
types of countertransference might be usefully disclosed,
when these disclosures are apt to prove useful, and how
one might state this material to the patient. The chapter

will be of a general and theoretical nature, with some brief case vignettes provided for illustration. More detailed case material will follow in later chapters.

Why Disclose Countertransference?

Before mentioning some of the aims and goals of those who advocate the selective disclosure of countertransferences, it is important to state the warnings against such disclosure. These warnings can be found not only in the work of "classical" analysts who maintain a classical definition of countertransference, but also in some of the writings of those who stress the value of countertransferential experiences.

Briefly stated, the principal arguments against open communication of countertransferential data include the belief that disclosure is apt to burden the patient or, alternatively, provide too great a gratification to him, and that it is therefore likely to confound or muddy the patient's transference to the analyst. In addition, it is argued that whatever purpose is sought in disclosing the countertransference can be attained by other means (exploring the patient's fantasies about the analyst's countertransference, for example), and thus the disclosure is unnecessary and apt to reflect the needs of the therapist and not those of the patient.

As one who advocates the selective disclosure of countertransferences, I am certain that all of these arguments apply much of the time. The open communication of countertransference *can* be a burden or provide excessive gratification, and it *can* reflect the therapist's countertransferential needs, such as for exoneration. Without indulging too greatly my own need for exoneration (I hope), let me say that I certainly have erred in these various ways with patients. The selective disclosure of countertransferences occasionally proved not to be selective enough. These errors can be costly, more costly perhaps than errors made in the interpretation of the patient's transferences or other material. Finding one's way back after an ill-timed or ill-conceived communication of countertransference can be quite difficult. Yet I believe a case can be made that the selective disclosure of countertransferences can accomplish, at times, some goals that are not as attainable, or not attainable at all, by any other means.

Why, then, disclose countertransference to the patient? Over the years, those who have advocated selective disclosure have done so for a variety of reasons. These reasons are typically presented in the context of a specific case or cases in which the therapist found it efficacious to communicate *some* of his feelings or fantasies to the patient; to my knowledge no serious writer on the subject has proposed that the therapist steadily and unselectively reveal countertransferences to the patient. From the early mavericks to some of the more recent proponents (Bollas 1983, Epstein 1979, Searles 1979, Spotnitz 1976, 1979), it has been emphasized that disclosures of countertransference must be made selectively and sparingly in order to have meaning and therapeutic traction.

In the work of these various investigators, the rationale for revealing countertransference is sometimes presented explicitly, while at other times it is merely implied. In general, though, the reasons for communicating countertransference are as follows: (1) the confirmation of the patient's sense of reality (Crowley 1952, Ferenczi 1931, 1933, Little 1951, 1957, Searles 1979, Winnicott 1949);

(2) the need to establish the therapist's honesty or genuineness (Epstein 1979, Kraemer 1957, Little 1951,
1957); (3) the need to establish the therapist's "humanness" and confirm the universality of transference,
thereby enabling the patient to more readily accept his
own humanness and transference (Colm 1955, Epstein
1979, Little 1957, Spotnitz 1976, 1979); (4) the need to
clarify both the fact and the nature of the patient's impact
on the therapist, and on people in general (Bollas 1983,
Ferenczi 1931, 1933, Little 1957, Spotnitz 1979, Winnicott 1949); and (5) on occasion, the need to end a treatment impasse or break through a deeply entrenched resistance (Bollas 1983, Colm 1955, Epstein 1979).

It will be noted that all of these reasons for disclosing
countertransferences are most clearly applicable to those
patients for whom a sense of basic trust, a sense of reality,
and clear-cut differentiation of self and object boundaries
is least firmly established—in short, those patients who
are more disturbed. And indeed, in most case illustrations
in which open communication of countertransference is
recommended, the focus is upon patients who would be
diagnosed as having psychotic, borderline, or narcissistic
disorders. This is not to say that disclosure is considered
inadvisable for healthier patients, such as neurotics and
patients with higher-level character disorders. Some investigators make it quite clear that they, at times, do openly
communicate some of their feelings and fantasies to these
patients as well (Bollas 1983, Little 1951, Spotnitz 1979).
It is in the treatment of patients with preoedipal disorders,
however, that investigators have found it most useful to
make known their countertransferences, for one or
another of the reasons just cited.

Apart from these specific reasons for communicating
countertransference, a fundamental overview regarding

the curative process in psychotherapy appears to guide
those who advocate disclosure. Stated quite simply, I believe these investigators share a similar notion about what
it is that makes people sick, and what it is that makes them
better. Namely, they stress the importance of real events
occurring in early childhood (actual deprivations and trau-
mas) as causative of illness, and they indicate that a real or
actual new experience with the therapist in the course of
treatment is an essential aspect of the curative process. In
this light, the selective communication of countertransference becomes a tool in the service of providing the patient
with this "new experience," one that is dissimilar from
that which actually occurred when the patient was a child.

Having outlined the rationale for communicating
countertransference, I will now turn to some of the situations in which disclosure appears useful. Two broad categories of such circumstances are (1) that in which the
countertransference has been acted out, or enacted, by the
therapist, and (2) that in which the countertransference is
experienced internally and evaluated, but not enacted, by
the therapist.

Disclosing Countertransference When Enactment Has Occurred

In considering various countertransference enactments, I
shall focus on three types: (1) that which is gross or
obvious, and whose occurrence is at once evident to both
therapist and patient; (2) that which is subtle, but whose
occurrence is consciously perceived and commented on by
the patient; (3) that which is subtle, and whose occurrence is primarily detectable by carefully monitoring the
patient's associations. Of these types, the subtle enact-

ments are probably more frequent and pervasive. The gross or obvious type occurs less often, though more often than one might wish. With all types, there is the important technical question as to what, if anything, can be usefully disclosed to the patient.

By gross or obvious enactments, I have in mind such actions as forgetting the patient's name, the time of the appointment, or the correct fee; or a slip of the tongue; or an evident lapse in the therapist's attention—in the extreme, even nodding off to sleep. I also have in mind certain uncontrolled and unintended displays of emotion by the therapist, such as a sudden exclamation of annoyance or exasperation. When these countertransferential enactments occur, the therapist may or may not have a quick sense as to their meaning. In either case, he is apt to feel that some statement is required from him. The question is, what kind of statement? There is almost universal agreement that the patient needs to receive from the therapist an acknowledgment that the enactment has occurred and, when appropriate, some statement of regret for its occurrence. But might the therapist say more? Here, there is a clear difference among therapists. Those who oppose open communication of countertransference would not say more. Reich states this point of view in no uncertain terms:

> To be sure, at times it may be unavoidable to admit certain countertransference manifestations to a patient; e.g., that the analyst forgot something or made a slip, etc. Such an admission may be required in order to permit the patient's free verbalization with regard to the analyst. But it is clearly quite a different matter to burden him with the analyst's own affairs and to interfere with the sequence of the analysis by

introducing extraneous material that is irrelevant for
the patient himself [1960, p. 390].

   Those who advocate the selective disclosure of countertransference, however, might offer more than a simple
"admission." One gathers that such proponents of disclosure as Ferenczi (see Thompson 1943) and Little (1951)
were inclined to reveal something of the cause of the
countertransferential enactment. They did not do so at all
times with all patients; rather, depending on the specific
situation, they might discuss—for some of the reasons
previously stated—the meaning of the enactment as they
understood it. I am essentially in agreement with this
approach. In my view, the therapist must be flexible in
technically handling these errors. A gross enactment that
might simply be acknowledged at one time, or to one
patient, could be usefully explored at another juncture or
with another patient.
   Perhaps an example or two will help to illustrate. Let
me take a particular error that I have made now and then:
I have forgotten to open my office door in time, thereby
effectively locking the patient out of my office.

   The first time this happened was with a relatively new
   patient, an attractive social work student with predominantly oedipal concerns. She was my first patient that day, and in forgetting to unlock the door I
   left her outside on a blustery autumn morning. She
   was at once struck by the error and said that she felt
   "locked out in the cold." Inasmuch as I had seen her
   only a few times, and also because I had little idea at
   the moment why I had forgotten to open the door
   (apart from my feeling vaguely ill and not wanting to
   work that day), I merely acknowledged that I had

forgotten to unlock the door and asked, "How do you feel about being locked out in the cold by me?" After quickly stating that she did not like it one bit, she went on to discuss her feelings of being "locked out in the cold" by men, including her boyfriend and an older brother whom she idolized as a child. At some point in the session I apologized for locking her out, but I did not disclose my motives for doing so—not my vague feeling of illness nor, when I later in the session realized it, my recognition that her seductiveness had temporarily unnerved me. Any mention of illness would likely have been experienced as a rationalization and would have made her even more frightened, on an unconscious level, of my ambivalent sexual countertransference to her. And any mention of my struggle with her seductiveness (a repetition, as it turned out, of her brother's reaction to her) at that time would have been a burden to her and might have short-circuited the evolution of her (brother) transference to me. In this instance, therefore, coming to grips with my feelings, as well as the "silent" use of this countertransferential data, appeared to be the wisest course.

By way of contrast, I recall locking out another patient—in this instance a borderline young man whom I had been treating for about a half year. During this time the patient had told me a good deal about himself and seemed to value coming for treatment, although he would frequently attempt to provoke me with some sort of personal attack. For the most part, I was unbothered by his remarks. One evening, however, his remarks were unusually vitriolic and did annoy me; what was even more irritating was his punctuating that evening by storming out of the session, flinging open the door and allowing the winter wind to blow through the office. The following session I inadvertently locked him out. When I did let him in, he commented dryly, "You want to keep me out tonight." He then continued in a low-key voice to speak of various rejections he had experienced that day at work. When he finished, I immediately returned to his initial comments and told him that, while I had not locked him out intentionally, in a way he was correct in thinking that I wanted to keep him out that night. I also told him why, stating, "Your unusually sharp remarks last session did annoy me. But what got to me even more was your taking out your anger by flinging the door open when you left. *That* really got me sore!" I then added, "I am sorry, though, that I evidently have taken out my anger by locking you out."

I believe that it was the disclosure of my own anger at him that was ultimately meaningful to him and made him sense, perhaps for the first time, his impact on me (Winnicott 1949); moreover, it enabled him to feel more comfortable in exploring his own provocativeness and hostility toward me (Epstein 1977). I do not believe a simple acknowledgment and apology for the obvious error would have been adequate. The patient needed to hear that I was angry at him and that I was aware that I, too, had acted it out.

   Gross or obvious countertransferential enactments, such as those just described, are bound to occur from time to time. But they are not as common as subtle enactments, which the patient may be either (1) consciously aware of, and state directly, or (2) unconsciously aware of, and reveal through associative material.

Analysts have long been aware of the importance of listening to the patient's commentary and associations for clues as to possible countertransferential enactments. In their early work, DeForest (1942) and Little (1951) both mention the importance of listening to the patient's material for indications of the analyst's countertransferential input. Among recent investigators, Langs (1976b, 1979, 1980) has paid special attention to the manifold ways in which the therapist's countertransferential enactments are processed and played back in the patient's associations. There has been no consensus, however, as to what, if anything, the therapist might disclose once he becomes aware, through either the patient's direct comments or his associative communications, that a countertransference enactment has occurred. Langs, for instance, indirectly acknowledges the occurrence but does not state explicitly any of his countertransferential feelings or fantasies. DeForest and Little, on the other hand, were inclined to selectively reveal a good deal, once they had understood the nature of their countertransferential input.

In agreement with DeForest and Little, I also find that it is occasionally helpful to disclose countertransferences in these kinds of situations. Before this can be done, however, the therapist must have some grasp of what he has inadvertently contributed to the interaction. It can be assumed that if the therapist has unknowingly enacted the countertransference, he is conflicted over some aspect of his feelings toward the patient. And because he is conflicted, it typically (though not always) will take some time before the therapist understands the full nature of his countertransference enactment. Nonetheless, some statement from him may still be in order. This is especially so when the patient says that he detects some countertransferential response in the therapist—and he is correct. Let us say, for example, that the patient picks up that the

therapist is irritated or annoyed with him, and the patient
expresses this directly. Assuming that the patient is correct, it is often necessary (after exploring the patient's
perception) to acknowledge that this is so. The therapist
may choose to add that he is not quite sure why he is
annoyed; or that he suspects he may be annoyed for such-
and-such a reason, but will have to think about it. What is
often essential for affirming the patient's sense of reality
testing and trust in the therapist's genuineness, is that the
therapist *does* confirm the patient's perception. (Technically, it is then necessary to explore the patient's reaction
to the therapist's disclosure.) For patients who struggled
with their parents' obfuscations and outright denials of
their emotional reactions to them when they were children, the therapist's confirmation of reality is fundamentally reassuring. At times, in fact, with more disturbed
patients, I have responded to what I sensed to be a patient's inaccurate evaluation of my countertransference in
this fashion: "Your perception that I am annoyed does not
seem accurate to me, but I will think about it." Or, "I am
not aware of being annoyed right now, but you have been
correct before, so I certainly will think about it."

In situations in which the therapist's recognition of a
countertransferential enactment is achieved through sensitively listening to the patient's associative material, he
may find it sufficient to note "silently" the patient's
unconscious perception and then "silently" work through
his own area of conflict. Sometimes, however, it may be
advisable to disclose some aspects of the countertransference, such as when the patient's associations (and his
own) lead the therapist to a relatively quick grasp of the
countertransference and the therapist has reason to believe that the patient can benefit from the disclosure. To
illustrate, let me take a common and specific form of

communication that often provides clues about countertransferential enactments: the patient's dreams about the
therapist or about a symbolic representative of the therapist. To be sure, dreams about the therapist reflect the
patient's transference patterns, but often they also provide clues as to how the therapist may unknowingly have
enacted aspects of the original object.

> In the termination phase of the treatment of a young
> woman with both narcissistic and depressive features,
> a dream of hers helped me discover and resolve a
> detrimental countertransference enactment. We both
> felt that the treatment, on the whole, had been suc-
> cessful. She had managed to extricate herself from
> the grasp of her narcissistic mother, and she felt
> secure in our relationship, stating that she felt
> "held" by me but not "suffocated," as she felt with
> her mother. I mention these details because they
> relate specifically to her dream during the termina-
> tion phase.
>   In her dream, she is in a circus performing on a
> trapeze. She is suddenly frightened, then falls, but is
> saved as she somersaults into the arms of a King
> Kong–like gorilla. The gorilla saves her, but when she
> wants to be let down so she can go away, he holds
> onto her tightly. She begins to feel suffocated.
>   She did not associate to the dream elements—as
> was her typical way of working—and instead began
> talking about the depressing weekend she had just
> spent with her mother. I did find myself associating
> to her dream, however, and quickly moved from "go-
> rilla" to my childhood nickname, "gorilla Gorkin,"
> and then to an association that may have been trig-
> gered by her talk about her mother—namely, that her

mother was, in more ways than one, an unusually "hairy" woman. These associations, among others, made it quite clear to me that I was the gorilla, whose hold, like her mother's, had become so tight that she could not get away. With this realization, I also had an awareness of how much I did not want her to get away, how much I would miss her, and then how I had inadvertently been enacting this countertransference by a subtle, depressive reaction to certain of her posttreatment plans.

Technically, I simply could have interpreted *her* perception of my gorilla-like grasp, silently resolving to work through my conflict. And I initially did restrict myself to an interpretation of her perception— which she reacted to by stating that she did feel "slightly suffocated" in treatment now, but she did not know why. It was then that I chose to give her the fuller interpretation. I told her that it was *my* perception also—that I, like her mother, had been feeling that I did not want her to go off, and in thinking over our recent sessions, I sensed my lack of enthusiasm (again paralleling her mother's response) for her posttreatment plans. This fuller interpretation led to a deluge of associative material, a further clarification of her relationship to her mother and to me, and eventually to a successful termination.

It could be argued that focusing only on *her* understanding of the transference-countertransference matrix, without my disclosure, could have led to a similar result. This is possible, though I will never know. My belief, however, is that the fuller interpretation infused our interaction with a greater vividness and meaningfulness than it might otherwise have had; further, linking my actual behavior to her mother's seemed to allow for the patient's richer understanding and acceptance not only of her own loss, but of mine *and* her mother's as well.

Disclosing Countertransference When Enactment Has Not Occurred

For the experienced therapist who has relatively free access to his own unconscious processes, as well as his conscious ones, awareness of the countertransference commonly precedes enactment. It is sometimes true, of course, that the mere disclosure of the countertransference becomes itself an enactment of that countertransference. For example, disclosure of the therapist's aggressive fantasies or feelings is, in part, an aggressive act. The difference between this form of enactment and the form discussed in the previous section is that here the therapist is conscious and in control of what he is doing. The therapist has been able to stand back and evaluate to what extent his countertransferential feelings and fantasies are personal and conflict-laden and to what extent they are an induced reaction, aroused within him by the impact of the patient's transference. Having evaluated the situation, which typically involves working through the personal or "subjective" aspect of the countertransference, the disclosure then issues from an assessment of the patient's needs. It is not a spontaneous reaction, but rather a calculated and modulated therapeutic act (or enactment).

One type of situation in which it can be advisable to disclose the countertransference is when an intractable resistance sets in, thereby jeopardizing the treatment. Even therapists who are usually opposed to disclosure will sometimes make a statement of countertransferential feelings in these circumstances. For instance, some violence-prone patients instill in the therapist considerable fear for his own safety. By means of projective identification, the patient engenders in the therapist the frightened, weak part of himself, and the therapist may feel quite paralyzed in his efforts to interpret anything that could provoke the patient. Several investigators have discussed this type of patient (Kernberg 1984, King 1976, Searles 1979) and have recommended that the therapist disclose his fear of the patient's potential violence. Quite obviously, the therapist cannot work effectively when he feels intimidated by the patient. When this kind of impasse occurs, there would seem to be no recourse other than to disclose one's predicament. The therapist's disclosure of his fear may provide the patient with a sense of triumph, but it also affords him the opportunity to explore his impact on other people. Above all, it provides the patient with a situation in which he can—indeed must—demonstrate the ability to control his aggressive impulses. To avoid disclosure in these situations is not helpful to the patient and may actually increase the chances of the patient's becoming violent with the therapist.

Another kind of impasse occurs when the patient, over a sustained period of time, refuses to take anything from the therapist; that is, the patient sets out to prove to himself and the therapist that the latter has nothing to offer him and that nothing can come of the treatment. This type of resistance pattern can be found among patients who are prone to counterdependency—some schizoid and narcissistic personalities, for example. In this situation, the therapist predictably feels a sense of futility and impotence. Interpretation of the patient's intentions often has no effect. Ironically, the only effective way out may be for the therapist to frankly disclose his feelings of impotence and ineffectiveness. The patient may experience a sense of triumph but, as is the case with the violence-prone patient, it gives him the opportunity to clarify his impact on others and provides a situation in which he can, and must, gain control over his destructiveness.

In the day-to-day practice of psychotherapy, treatment impasses of this type are relatively uncommon. Yet the treatment need not be in such jeopardy before the therapist discloses something of the impact of the patient's transference on him. There are a variety of situations in which selective disclosure of the countertransference can help the patient sense how he comes across to others and can help him repossess or reintroject that part of himself which he has extruded and engendered in the other (therapist). This is most true in the treatment of more disturbed patients, although it occasionally applies to healthier patients as well. Consider some brief examples.

Perhaps the most frequently cited use of disclosure is in those situations in which the therapist is beset by "hateful" feelings toward the patient (Epstein 1977, Spotnitz 1976, Winnicott 1949). This is a common development in the treatment of psychotic and borderline patients. The patient, by means of projective identification, engenders in the therapist some unwanted, noxious part of himself, and the therapist is left to struggle with this internal experience.

For instance, in the treatment of the provocative borderline young man whom I inadvertently locked out of the office, the projection of a provoked, intruded-upon part of himself was central to his transferential manner of relating to me. In essence, he was doing to me what his mother had done to him. As it happened, I was initially unable to contain and metabolize his projection. My con-

flict over my own aggression toward him, and specifically
my anger at being intruded upon, led to a spontaneous,
uncontrolled countertransference enactment. It would
have been better to let him know something about my
reaction to him at a time of my own choosing—that is,
after I had understood and metabolized this aggression. I
do believe, however, that it eventually would have been
necessary to let him know that I was aware of his attempts
to provoke me and, what is more, that I did feel provoked
and annoyed by him. Interpretation of his transference
alone, without some disclosure of the countertransference, would likely make the patient feel that I was too
removed from him, perhaps even that I was somehow
"above" him. The patient needed to know that he affected
me, but he did not overwhelm me. My ability to absorb
and metabolize the internal experience of being provoked
and intruded upon could then be available to him for
reintrojection (Malin and Grotstein 1966, Ogden 1979).
The danger of the crude enactment of locking him out of
the office was that I had indicated, temporarily, that I *had*
been overwhelmed by my countertransferential feelings.
The willingness to honestly acknowledge what had happened was an initial and vital step in regaining some
control over my aggression, and this did help him. But, as
stated, the most effective technical approach would have
been to provide, at an appropriate time, an interpretation
of the transference *and* countertransference, without any
crude enactment. Chapter 7 will further consider the issue
of the therapist's disclosure of countertransferential aggression in the treatment of borderline patients.

Another example of the use of countertransference
disclosure as a means of highlighting the transference
occurs in the treatment of healthier patients, for whom
interpretation of transference alone might seem sufficient.

In working with patients who are characterologically passive, for instance, the therapist is likely to find himself tempted to become more active. He may ask more questions or make more clarifications and interpretations. In such a situation, I have sometimes found it useful not only to point out the patient's transferential manner of relating, but also to disclose that I came to sense this pattern through an awareness of my temptation to jump in and do something or say something—that is, to become the active one in the room.

With a healthier patient who has an adequate observing ego, it is generally possible to interpret only the patient's transferential manner of relating—in this case, the patient's passivity and way of inviting others to take over. Such an interpretation could be expected to lead to an insightful awareness on the patient's part. If the therapist includes a statement of the countertransference as part of the interpretation of the transference, however, the patient's impact on others can sometimes be rendered more immediate and vivid. Beyond this, the therapist's disclosure of his feelings in this type of situation can have a subtly beneficial influence on the working alliance between therapist and patient. It helps contribute to the patient's sense that the therapist is in there working, even struggling, with him. By disclosing aspects of the countertransference as part of some routine transference interpretations, even in the treatment of healthier patients, the therapist may be able to give the interpretation an even greater value, without encumbering the patient with an unnecessary burden or gratification.

It will be noted that in the previously described situations in which the therapist discloses the countertransference (and no enactment has occurred), he does so after he has obtained a clear understanding of its nature and

source. This understanding may come quickly, but it is
more often a matter of days, weeks, even months before
the therapist feels he has a thorough grasp of the transference-countertransference matrix.

It is generally advisable for the therapist to wait until
he has such an understanding before he opts for disclosure. But sometimes, and with some patients, it can be
useful for the therapist to reveal a countertransferential
reaction that may not yet be entirely clear to him. For
example, the therapist may find it useful to state a vague
feeling—for example, a sense of disconnectedness that he
has recently noticed between himself and the patient—
and wonder aloud if the patient has any thoughts about it.
Or, the therapist might mention a visual fantasy or an
association that he senses is connected to what the patient
just reported, even though he, the therapist, is not yet
clear about the connection. In so doing, the therapist is
providing a clue (which is all he has), and not a well-
formulated statement or interpretation. He invites the
patient to help provide some of the remaining details, to
fill in the gaps. Of course, if the statement is poorly timed,
the therapist runs the risk of frightening the patient, or of
encouraging him to engage in the blood sport of analyzing
the analyst. However, this type of disclosure sometimes
deepens both therapist's and patient's understanding, and
enhances the working alliance and the patient's sense of
the therapist's genuine participation.

This particular use of countertransference disclosure
is lucidly discussed in Bollas's excellent contribution "Ex-
pressive Uses of the Countertransference" (1983), and it
is suggested in several of the essays in the book *Countertransference*, edited by Epstein and Feiner (1979). The
latter authors represent the Sullivanian interpersonal

school, and it is perhaps among the interpersonalists that this kind of countertransference disclosure has been most thoroughly explored and advocated.

Some Additional Noninterpretative Forms of Countertransference Disclosure

Some types of countertransference disclosure do not involve—at least initially—the use of interpretation, but rather rely on deliberate, usually modulated, enactments of the countertransference. In this type of disclosure, the therapist consciously chooses to enact in some measure the countertransference that has been engendered in him. He chooses this form of disclosure because he believes that an enactment is needed in order to effectively "speak to" the patient or in order to render the patient capable of hearing a subsequent interpretation. It is almost exclusively for use with severely disturbed patients—psychotics and borderlines—that this technical procedure has been recommended. And what has been engendered and then deliberately enacted by the therapist is generally some type of negative or aggressivized countertransference.

A negative or aggressivized countertransference can be deliberately enacted in various ways. For example, the therapist can let the patient know of his negative or aggressive feelings by stating them, directly and emotionally. This technique, as practiced by some therapists (Little 1957, Searles 1979, Spotnitz 1963), makes use of the therapist's genuine, but modulated, negative countertransference. Those who advocate this use of the therapist's feelings (as I do) believe that this may be the most effective way of enabling some severely disturbed patients to realize and accept their own negative or aggressive transferences, as well as the real (not fantasized) impact of these transferences on the therapist. Interpretation, if it is to have any value, must follow the actual verbal enactment of the transference-countertransference matrix.

The therapist can engage in a form of role playing as a variation of this technical use of countertransference enactment. Having evaluated and metabolized the induced countertransference, the therapist then dramatizes the engendered feelings or role. The style of the dramatization can vary considerably, from a loud, hyperbolic dramatization of the countertransference to a paradoxical dramatization, played out in a dry, matter-of-fact manner. Typically, it is a negative or aggressivized countertransference experience which the therapist chooses to enact.

The principal proponents of this technical use of countertransference belong to the "modern" psychoanalytic school, founded by Spotnitz. Their journal, *Modern Psychoanalysis*, has presented many papers over the last decade in which this noninterpretative use of countertransference is demonstrated, above all, in the treatment of severely disturbed patients.

A simple example, mentioned by Spotnitz (1963), occurred in the treatment of a "highly narcissistic" patient who occasionally taunted him with absurd threats. Unconsciously, the patient was frightened of his own aggression, believing himself to be unique in his destructiveness, and thus uniquely evil. By relating in this taunting fashion, the patient did in fact arouse considerable counteraggression in the therapist. Spotnitz chose to dramatically enact this aggressivized countertransference. One day, when the patient said he was thinking of "bashing in" Spotnitz's head, Spotnitz countered vehemently,

"No you won't, because I'll bash in yours before you get off the couch" (p. 89).

Spotnitz argues that by enacting the countertransference in this dramatic fashion, he initiated a process whereby the patient was eventually able to accept the full extent of his own aggressive transference. The patient was able to make such progress because he no longer felt like he was the only one in the world—or in the room—with such destructive impulses; he realized moreover, that it was possible to have such destructive impulses, experience them, state them, without acting on them. It is assumed, of course, that the patient was aware that Spotnitz would not actually enact his threat to bash in the patient's head.

Let us next consider an example of a countertransference enactment played out in a paradoxical manner. A borderline patient, frightened of her unconscious hostility toward the therapist (who in the transference stands for the hated part of her self), expresses this hostility by means of a subtle denigration of the therapist. Nothing he says is quite right, quite good enough, or quite useful. The therapist is made to feel useless and worthless; that is, he is made to experience the devalued part of the patient's self. Instead of providing an interpretation of this interaction—which he believes the patient will not hear—the therapist dramatically enacts his countertransference. He agrees with the patient that it must be difficult to be in treatment with such an incompetent, unskilled therapist; he can sympathize with her. He adds that it is a shame to be throwing away such good money on this therapy, which is really nonsense and going nowhere. All this is stated in a dry, matter-of-fact tone and is continued until the patient becomes so fed up that she explodes in open and direct anger, which the therapist also absorbs and accepts without recrimination.

This paradoxical technique, sometimes referred to as "joining the resistance" (Spotnitz 1976), has a specific aim. As in the first example, the goal is to enable the patient to experience the full extent of her warded-off hatred, as well as the fact that the therapist can bear this hatred without being overwhelmed by it. In addition, inasmuch as the therapist in this example has become projectively identified as the embodiment of the devalued part of the patient's self, acceptance on his part of this projection (conveyed by the matter-of-fact tone, not by his words), is then available to the patient for reinternalization.

These role-playing dramatizations of countertransference are not practiced by many analysts. Indeed, the vast majority would undoubtedly consider such techniques a crass, destructive manipulation of the patient. It is not my purpose here to advocate this brand of countertransference disclosure; I believe that the use of these measures can easily convert the analytic situation into a form of game playing, rather then a genuine human encounter. Nonetheless, I do believe that, on rare occasions, when everything else has failed, it may be of some value to attempt a dramatization of the countertransference. With some severely disturbed and highly resistant patients, a dramatization may be worth a try, but I would not recommend the wider use of these interventions, as suggested by the modern analytic school.

— 5 —

Varieties of Sexualized Countertransference

I shall begin this chapter by presenting a clinical vignette that, in a somewhat unsettling manner, first alerted me to the therapeutic value of sexualized counter-transference.

I had been working for several months with a 10-year-old boy, M., whose presenting symptom, as described by the mother, was a slackening in school work shortly after her divorce from M.'s father. The mother had custody of all three children: an older brother, M., and a younger sister. M. shrugged off any sadness or anger about the divorce and seemed to enter into the therapeutic relationship easily and openly. He drew pictures, usually of pirates and Superman-like figures, and he had a rather typical enthusiasm for playing "war" with plastic soldiers. He also was an ardent Yankee baseball fan; in fact, with the possible exception of the TV announcers, I can-

not imagine anyone knowing more of the statistics—
he called them "stats"—on the players.

I highlight M.'s boyish interests because in spite
of them, I gradually found myself reacting to him in
ways I might have reacted to an alluring girl: as cute,
endearingly charming, and above all, seductively cud-
dlesome. At times I wanted to throw my arms about
him, squeeze him tight, give him a kiss. I felt him to
be a lovely young girl. In attempting to sort out for
myself whence this reaction came, I began to pay
closer attention to the subtleties of M.'s interaction
with me. I then began to notice how his movements
at times had a kind of furtive quality to them. He
occasionally would walk and almost brush up against
me, cat-like. Also, some of his gestures, while not
effeminate, took on a seductive cast—for example, a
lingering look and slow running of his hand through
his hair as he hesitated near the door at the end of the
session.

Alerted by my countertransference to M., I
began in the course of my sessions with the mother to
question her on more of the details of M.'s family
relationships. It was then that she recalled that M.
had always been very jealous of his younger sister,
who, as it turns out, was the father's favorite. Moreover, she remembered that when M. was a small boy
he had often wanted to dress up in her clothing,
although he had given this up when he entered
school. She thought at the time that there was something "vaguely homosexual" about this, but she no
longer worried about him. M., after all, had become
"a real boy, a terrific athlete and baseball player."

It would take me too far afield to describe in any
detail the course of M.'s three years of therapy with me.

Suffice it to say that his sexual identity was substantially confused, and much work had to be done in this area. I believe that this issue would have become clear to me eventually even had I not been aware of my initial countertransferential response, and especially my sexual fantasy, toward M. as a seductive young girl. But my fantasy did prove to be an early, poignant, and accurate gauge of M.'s inner conflict. What is more, I found my countertransferential response useful throughout the therapy, particularly in gauging the progression, and at times regression, in M.'s therapeutic development. Finally, and perhaps most crucially, my awareness of the countertransference was of considerable help in preventing me from subtly acting out M.'s wish (and mine). Without this awareness it is likely that I would have unwittingly encouraged the perpetuation of, or brought about the premature renunciation of, M.'s (and my) wish for him to be a lovely young girl.

The Concept of
Sexualized Countertransference

Before exploring in a systematic way some of the types of sexualized countertransference, we must establish the meaning of the phrase. As M.'s case indicates, what interests me is the responses that arise, more or less predictably, as a reaction to the patient's transference. Thus, by *sexualized countertransference* I am referring here to that gamut of sexual feelings and fantasies that is evoked in the therapist by any of a wide variety of sexualized transferences. These sexual feelings and fantasies may be of an oral, anal, phallic, or genital nature. Furthermore, just as the patient's sexualization of the transference may be in the service of aims other than purely erotic ones—narcissistic needs and hostile wishes, for example—so is the sexualization of the countertransference often reflective of the therapist's other aims.

I prefer to call this type of countertransference "sexualized" and not "erotized" because, as will be discussed in more detail later, the term *erotized* has traditionally been linked with a singular type of transference, known as the "erotized transference" (Blum 1973, Greenson 1967, Langs 1974, Rappaport 1956), meaning an egosyntonic and near-delusional demand on the part of the patient for sexual relations with the therapist. I do not want to restrict my discussion to those countertransference reactions that are evoked by this small, albeit important, category of patients. For that reason, as well as to avoid any semantic confusion, I prefer the term *sexualized*.

It is worth noting that, in spite of the burgeoning interest in countertransference issues, scant attention has been paid in the literature to the therapist's sexual feelings and fantasies toward patients. One can only speculate as to the reasons for this. I do not think it is primarily a matter of therapists' repression of their sexual fantasies, although one does sometimes have the impression that it is more comfortable nowadays for a therapist to fantasize throwing a patient out of the office than it is to imagine joining the patient on the couch. Still, in today's more liberal milieu, with the growing acceptance of the clinical importance of countertransference, it is impossible to believe that therapists are unaware of their sexual fantasies and feelings about their patients.

Rather, what I think has happened is that we have probably paid too little attention to the vicissitudes of our sexual fantasies and feelings because our focus has been elsewhere. The clinical material that originally spawned, and continues to nurture, analytic interest in countertransference has been the treatment of preoedipal patients. Much of the seminal work on countertransference (Little 1951, 1957, Winnicott 1949), as well as the more recent explorations (Epstein and Feiner 1979, Searles 1979, Spotnitz 1976), have been concerned with the uses of countertransference with severe character disorders and psychotics. Therapists who treat such patients have had to struggle with, first and foremost, a panoply of aggressive countertransferential reactions. In addition, precisely because these patients are more severely disturbed—that is, preoedipal—many of the investigators who took up an interest in countertransference matters understandably found themselves deemphasizing oedipal issues. And along with this deemphasis on oedipal issues came a deemphasis on sexual issues in general. Therapists found themselves less concerned with the vicissitudes of the sexual instincts in these patients—often of a polymorphous perverse nature—and more concerned with the swings of aggression toward self and others. I do not want to quarrel with this emphasis. What I do suggest is that it has ultimately led to a preponderance of interest in aggressivized countertransferences, with a corresponding tendency to overlook or underrate the usefulness of sexualized countertransference in the treatment of both oedipal and preoedipal patients.

The primary exception to this trend can be found in Racker's (1953, 1957) early, bold, and almost encyclopedic efforts to systematize countertransference reactions. Operating from the assumption that "we are still children and neurotics even when we are adults and analysts" (1957, p. 307), Racker examined some forms of sexualized countertransference. He was concerned with the therapist's countertransferential "predispositions," which issue from the neurotic vestiges of the therapist's Oedipus complex (1953, pp. 314-317). Seen in this light, female patients are in some measure reacted to as the therapist's oedipal mother, and male patients as the oedipal father; and, of course, both positive and negative oedipal complexes come into play. My view is that Racker was both correct and illuminating as far as he went. Yet, on the whole, he was less interested in delineating these sexual countertransferences than in exploring those countertransference issues pertinent to the "depressive" and "paranoid" positions. Also, as will be indicated in some of the clinical vignettes that follow, one simply cannot squeeze all types or manifestations of sexualized countertransference into the theoretical straightjacket of the Oedipus complex.

Apart from Racker's work, there has been only an occasional paper, or mention within a paper, of sexualized countertransference. Searles (1979), for example, in discussing his treatment of schizophrenic and borderline patients, has briefly but clearly articulated some of his more rambunctious sexual fantasies and feelings toward these patients. A few additional investigators have commented on the occasional emergence of sexual feelings in the course of treating some patients (Davis 1978, Kohrman et al. 1971, Marshall 1979). Yet those observations stand in contrast to the principal trend within the analytic community (or communities), which has been to focus on our aggression, and not our sexual responses, toward patients.

The rest of this chapter will delineate some of the types of sexualized countertransference that occur in the course of therapy with various kinds of patients, including (1) patients (females) with erotized transference, (2) hysterics (females), (3) masochists (females), and (4) phallic characters (females and males). These diagnostic labels are necessarily mere generalizations, and this discussion is thus meant to be somewhat general; individual differences, of course, do come into play. Finally, it will be noted that I am discussing sexualized countertransference solely from the perspective of the male therapist. Obviously, this is the vantage point that is most accessible to me. But I believe that analogous situations exist for female therapists, although no doubt with some variations in emphasis on one aspect or another of the countertransferential theme.

The Erotized Transference in Females

In a paper that was both witty and wise, Freud (1915) first began to discuss erotized transference, although he did not specifically designate it as such. Describing the type of woman (he did not consider the possibility in men) who developed an erotized transference, he wrote:

> These are women of elemental passionateness who tolerate no surrogates. They are children of nature who refuse to accept the psychical in place of the material, who in the poet's words, are accessible only to "the logic of soup, with dumplings for aguments." With such people one has the choice between returning their love or else bringing down upon oneself the full enmity of a woman scorned. In neither case can one safeguard the interests of the treatment. One has to withdraw, unsuccessful; and all one can do is to turn the problem over in one's mind of how it is that a capacity for neurosis is joined with such an intractable need for love [pp. 166–167].

Since Freud's initial observations, the term *erotized transference* has been used to designate a specific type of transference manifestation: the egosyntonic demand for

sex with the therapist. Patients manifesting this transference are generally described not in terms of "elemental
passionateness," but rather in the context of severe ego
pathology—that is, as psychotic, borderline, or narcissistic (Blum 1973, Greenson 1967, Langs 1974, Rappaport
1956). Significantly, none of the investigators has delineated the countertransference experiences that are expectable when faced with such an onslaught of sexualized
wishes and demands. There is an occasional suggestion
that the erotized transference can be repellent to the
therapist. Apart from such observations, however, these
investigators have limited themselves to admonishments
that the therapist need be especially wary not to encourage
the patient in her delusional demand for sex.

In my view, there is a good deal more that can—and
must—be said about the countertransference to these patients. Unfortunately, I must limit my remarks to females
because I have never treated a male in whom there has
been an erotized transference. First, we must ask whether
the therapist's distaste for, or repulsion by, the erotized
transference is, in itself, a countertransference resistance—specifically, a defense against being tempted by the
sexual invitations of the patient. I doubt whether this
factor carries much weight. Rather, I believe it is, up to a
point, an expectable countertransferential reaction when
faced with the patient's attempt to destroy the treatment.
Her offer of sex and love is also, in part, an accusation that
the therapist's way of doing things is useless. A negative
response—distaste, repulsion—is predictable in light of
the underlying hostility toward the therapist.

Still, we must ask whether the therapist might not
also be expected to have a sexual response to the erotized
transference. I have found that a sexual countertransfer-

ence has usually emerged; furthermore, I have found it useful in understanding these patients.

A patient of mine in her mid-20s, K., developed an erotized transference in the second year of her four-year-long treatment. Dressed in carefully matched, skin-tight outfits, K. frequently professed a wish to seduce me. At times, it seemed as if she came to her sessions primarily to accomplish this aim. K. did not talk easily and was in fact quite schizoid, although in the course of her years with me she did tell her sad story; the most poignant and important detail of which involved the death of her tyranically protective mother when K. was 11 years old.

At first, K.'s openly expressed wishes to be held, kissed, fondled, and penetrated were simply offputting to me. Although I kept my negative reactions to myself, I eagerly wished she would renounce these demands or, better yet, look at them as part of our analytic passion play. But they persisted in elemental force. As time went on I found myself, in turn, having sexual fantasies about her, wishing to do to her more or less what she wanted. I communicated none of this to her. I silently observed my counter-transference, and I noticed that these sexual fantasies took on for me a deep wish to rescue her. A part of my ego accepted her demand, her argument, that if only I would have sex with her she could get better, and unless I did, she would never get better. The other part of my ego, the analyzing part, knew full well that this was folly. But the part of my ego that was locked into this fusion fantasy with her had become hooked, and it was then that I noticed another fantasy taking shape. I wished to have sex with her not simply to rescue her, but to rescue *me*. It would cure *me*. It is difficult to put this raw experience into words, but it was something of the order that I would be made whole and totally vital if only— and only if—I had sex with K.

In evaluating this primitive transference-countertransference matrix, I came to understand that for K. the desire for sex with me was the clearest, and perhaps the only, way she could communicate her yearning for contact with me—as a vital, nurturant, and ultimately symbiotic mother. It was this early contact that had been disrupted when her mother left her to go off to work when she was an infant, and that was symbolically repeated in her mother's death. In arousing my sexual wishes toward her, she was arousing my omnipotent and grandiose wish to be the all-good, symbiotic mother to her. As for *my* desire to be rescued by her, I believe it was activated by her wish, also omnipotent and grandiose, to be curative toward me, much as she still wished to make her idealized mother alive again, and much as she earlier had wished to make her mother supply the symbiotic oneness that had been prematurely disrupted. In sum, our mutual sexual fantasies were fundamentally in the service of recreating a Garden of Eden, a symbiotic oneness. They were for me, and I believe for K. too, more desperate than enticing. They were hardly ever fun.

Searles (1979) has described a wide variety of countertransferential phenomena that occur in the treatment of primitive mental disorders. Although not dwelling at any length on sexualized countertransference, he notes how in the therapist's regression the wish to be curative toward the patient can take on the primitive urge to do so sexually. He writes: "It has long been my impression that a major reason for therapists' becoming actually sexually involved with patients is that the therapist's own therapeutic striving, desublimated to the level on which it was at work early in his childhood, has impelled him into this form of involvement with the patient. He has succumbed to the illusion that a magically curative copulation will resolve the patient's illness which tenaciously has resisted all the more sophisticated psychotherapeutic techniques learned in adult-life training and practice" (p. 431).

I agree with this observation. But my experience with K. and others has made it clear to me that the therapist also sometimes regressively wishes to be the one who is magically cured. While not specifically pointing this out, Searles's conception of the patient's need to be therapist to his analyst is in keeping with this view. In short, the "magically curative copulation" is desired by both, and for the same reason: to cure and be cured. The cure here is also magically elaborated by both. It is a cure in the form of a renaissance, in which an all-good oneness is reestablished. Mutual hostility is denied.

The mere experience of this form of sexualized countertransference need not lead to sexual acting out. The therapist's awareness of these induced feelings can help him know the patient and formulate interpretations to her. In addition, by sinking but not drowning in the countertransference, part of the therapist's ego remains aware of the "magical" nature of the copulation. This awareness helps the therapist avoid not only actual sexual activity with the patient, but also the more subtle forms that sexual acting out generally takes. Along with Searles, I would agree that when sexual activity does in fact occur, we may be sure that omnipotent and grandiose fantasies have overtaken both patient and therapist. As a corollary, one notes that actual sexual involvement is most unlikely with healthier, oedipal-level patients.

The Female Hysteric

If there is one patient that (male) therapists almost universally seem to enjoy treating, it is a "good" (female) hysteric. With a mixture of wistfulness and envy—no doubt oedipally inspired—we imagine that our predecessors in the field treated a greater number of these "good" hysterics. Emotionally responsive and intuitive, they come into treatment frightened but excitedly expectant. Underestimating their own capacities, they are ready to overvalue those of the therapist. The therapist need do nothing other than be his analyzing self, and the hysteric will readily develop a warmly idealizing, romantic transference. Such a transference carries its own set of problems—some of which will be explored here—but as transferences go, this one is relatively pleasant to treat.

Although much has been written about the treatment of hysterics, very little has been said about the countertransference that develops in response to them. Freud (1915) does speculate about "a woman's subtler and aim-inhibited wishes which bring with them the danger of making a man forget his technique and medical task for the sake of a fine experience" (p. 170). But he does not apply this observation specifically to hysterics. Moreover, Freud views this countertransference as more of an interference than a tool in the analytic work.

My observation is that a useful and somewhat predictable type of sexualized countertransference develops, and its features are a response to the transference of the female hysteric. By way of comparison, we note that, unlike the more regressed patient who develops an erotized transference, the hysteric makes a concentrated effort to avoid the emergence of sexual feelings toward the therapist. Frightened by the dangers of her sexuality, she represses the emergence of sexual feelings toward this person, this man, whom she admires and respects. At the same time, by suggestion, by indirection, by her tone and gesture, she creates an atmosphere that is replete with romanticism and sentimentality. And in all this, with a hand that knows not what it is doing, she lets fall the handkerchief of sexuality. The therapist's problem is whether, and when, and how to pick it up.

A common countertransference problem engendered by this type of patient is that the therapist similarly becomes timid of, and in various ways attempts to avoid, a sexualized countertransference. The therapist attempts to evade his sexual fantasies and feelings toward the patient just as she evades her fantasies and feelings toward him.

I recall working with an attractive 31-year-old woman who by the end of her first year in treatment had formed a warmly idealizing transference. She had never reported a sexual fantasy about me, and she was also cautiously tangential in describing sexual experiences with her boyfriend. She had let the handkerchief of sexuality drop in subtle ways, but I never picked it up; I never interpreted it. Instead, I began to notice within myself warm feelings and fantasies about touching and caressing her, but I attempted to suppress these wishes. I had the urge to smell the perfumed pillow after she left, to watch her as she walked up the stairs. There was a sense of sweet

forbiddenness to all this, even as I strenuously attempted to rid myself of the thoughts. It soon became
obvious to me, though, that I was dealing with my
sexual fantasies precisely as she unconsciously dealt
with hers and, moreover, that I was probably repeating what her once-playful father had done as she
approached the oedipal stage, and again as she entered puberty.

I did not communicate this countertransferential data to her directly. After processing it internally,
however, I was able to discuss with her some of her
sexual fears, as well as their historical context, in a
way that was neither coolly interpretive nor too seductive. This ultimately led to a clearing of her resistance to experiencing sexual material in greater
depth, both in her life and in the transference.

I believe that this air of temptation and forbiddenness
that attaches to the sexual countertransference with hysterics is rather common. It is fundamentally linked to the
oedipal experience in both patient and therapist. For the
male therapist, his positive oedipal wishes toward his
mother come into play with this kind of female patient—a
point discussed by Racker (1953). Again, in comparison
with the sexualized countertransference in cases of erotized transference, it is not accompanied by feelings of
heroic rescue. Rather it is, as Freud phrased it, the wish
for a "fine experience," albeit a forbidden one.

Recognition of one's attempt to avoid or suppress the
sexualized countertransference can provide useful information about the patient and her history. Even more
important, it can help the therapist avoid unproductive
and destructive evasions of this countertransference. One
obvious countertransference evasion is that the therapist

becomes overly hesitant about picking up the dropped handkerchief of sexuality, thereby, under the guise of understanding, causing further repression. In doing this, the therapist runs the risk of repeating, as with my patient, the experience of the coolly withdrawn father. The patient unconsciously understands that her sexuality is threatening to the therapist, and it therefore never emerges in the force necessary for a complete analytic working-through to occur.

Another kind of problem that can develop when the therapist avoids the conscious experience of sexual feelings about the patient is that he unconsciously acts them out. He can do this by behaving seductively toward the patient, in a manner that would be obvious to an outside observer. The result of this more overt seductiveness is that the hysteric becomes frightened, generally on an unconscious level, of her potentially dangerous and incestuous wishes. Her repression is thus solidified. As a rule, however, our training and professionalism steer us away from the more obvious and overt forms of seductiveness.

But there is a type of covert seductiveness to which we are especially susceptible—a type that is reinforced by our training. It is the seductiveness of our role as the interpreter, the possessor of psychological knowledge. The hysteric, perhaps more than any other type of patient, experiences the process of making *known* her sexual feelings and fantasies, in precisely the biblical sense of that verb; that is, to reveal this material to the therapist is felt by her to be, in itself, an act of sexual intimacy. As long as the therapist steers clear of the patient's explicitly sexual motives, he may indicate through his comments and interpretations that he knows her. However, once this explicit sexual material is interpreted, the therapist's knowledge frequently takes on a dangerous "phallic" meaning. The hysteric recoils. The therapist is then in danger of being tempted to return to the role of kindly seer, whose knowledge is supposedly not of forbidden fruit. Or, as can easily happen, the therapist may persist with his "phallic" interpretations. The patient is then likely to experience him as frighteningly seductive. She rejects his interpretations and this rejection, in turn, can precipitate a negative reaction on the part of the therapist toward the patient.

I have found that my safest guide to not entering into these destructive interactions is the conscious recognition of my sexualized countertransference toward the patient. By accepting my feelings and fantasies, I find that the danger of acting out or evading them is thereby diminished. I am able then to work through my sexualized countertransference with that particular patient, at that particular time.

The Female Masochist

Over the years, masochism has been examined from a number of perspectives, each with its own corner on the truth. The classical position, outlined by Freud (1919), is to regard masochism as an oedipally based disorder in which the masochist suffers from guilt over incestuous wishes. Subsequent investigators have sought to link masochism with other characterological disorders in which both oedipal and preoedipal features play a part—paranoid character traits (Nydes 1963), depression (Kernberg 1975), and narcissism (Stolorow and Lachmann 1980), for example. While it is beyond the intent of this chapter to fully enter this diagnostic controversy, I do want to indicate the type of masochism to which I am referring. I have in mind those patients, primarily female, whose sexual feelings and fantasies toward the therapist, and others, take on a pronounced character of punishment and injury to the self, and in whom these wishes issue from both oedipal and preoedipal concerns.

Most commonly, I have found that these women have had an actual experience, with a father, brother, or other older male, in which sexual excitement was mingled with punishment. Furthermore, this punishing but exciting interaction was the most reliable and consistent form of receiving attention and contact from the particular older male. Thus the masochistic wish served a narcissistic function and also provided, though inevitably in a self-defeating manner, temporary relief from depression.

There are masochistic males who exhibit analogous backgrounds. Generally, as Freud (1919) noted, their masochism occurs in the context of sensing themselves as feminine. I have not addressed these cases because my experience of treating female masochists is more extensive. In addition, I wish to distinguish female masochists from female hysterics. Hysterics also, at times, exhibit masochistic fantasies, but their fantasies are accompanied more by a wish to experience the man's power and strength than a wish to be injured and humiliated. In the masochist, punishment and woundedness are far more entwined as part of the sexual experience.

It is my observation that the sexualized transference of the masochistic female typically engenders within the male therapist a corresponding type of reaction: She induces an aggressive or sadistic sexualized countertransference. With such patients, the therapist may attempt to evade his sadistic feelings by becoming overly benign and kindly. This evasion is the exact analogue of what the patient herself will often do in order to avoid her transference. In other words, the patient and/or therapist attempt to be very, very good in order not to be horrid. Alternatively, the therapist may respond to the masochistic inducements by unwittingly indulging his sadism. This may be accomplished in any number of ways, including a tendency toward becoming provocative or coolly withholding, by adding some bite to one's interpretations, or by a more-than-usual probing of the patient's associations. All of these types of subtle acting out, as well as the evasion of excessive kindliness, often represent resistances to the conscious experience of a sadistic sexualized countertransference.

   I have occasionally found that it has taken me a long while with a patient before the sexualized countertransference becomes conscious. And unfortunately, by that time, I have already blundered into a number of evasions or subtle types of acting out.

   I remember, for instance, a 22-year-old woman, B., whose presenting problem was simply one of occasional anxiety attacks. B. had been married for two years, happily she thought. Before then, there had been "only a meaningless affair or two, nothing very much." B.'s manner was quiet and sweet, so sweet that I managed to overlook the portentousness of her first dream. This dream, told with a sense of girlish embarrassment, involved a scene at the home where she was raised along with her two older brothers. In the backyard of that home, the family wash was hanging out to dry. Her bra and panties were noticeable among the clothing on the line. This dream fragment produced no associations, and when I mentioned something about washing one's dirty linen in public, B. shrugged it off with an air of insouciance.
   There were few other dreams in the months

following this initial fragment, and B. seemed to find it difficult to talk of her life or anyone in it. Eventually she did begin to discuss her husband, her family, and her work. Yet she did this in the most cursory way, *unless* I began to probe for details. In fact, that became our pattern: B. would offer up a piece of information, then remain silent, and I would hunt for details. My clue that I had entered into something of a morass with her was that I began to feel, during these probings, a sense of being teased. I also felt I was forcing myself upon her, and, in a sense, I was.

I gave up this hyperinquisitiveness—though I was at the time not sure of its underlying meaning— only to find myself engaged in a new form of acting out with her. This was a year and a half into the treatment, and B. had begun to warm up to me. Her warming, however, took on the aspect of a flirtatious baiting, and I found myself joining in, needling her back. It was during one of our exchanges that I noticed the emergence of sadistic sexual fantasies toward her. I wished to take her clothes off, tear them off, and grab her all over. These fantasies were attended less by warm feelings than by a sense of using her. Sadistically, I imagined how much she would like it, even though she would tell me to stop. I did not tell B. any of this, but instead waited for a relaxed moment, at which time I drew her attention to the teasing pattern of our exchanges. It was soon after this observation that B. finally revealed her dark secret: She had been incestuously involved with her brother. From the age of 11 to 13, she had frequent sexual contact with this older brother, whose first name, as it happened, was the same as mine. They had never had intercourse, but B. had submitted, at first reluctantly, to his requests to fondle her. Later she had often teased him into it. She also began to reveal with great shame her numerous fantasies of having sex with me, all of which involved my forcing her to do something against her will and ended in her humiliation.

I feel certain that, had I been more immediately aware of my sexualized countertransference, I would not have acted provocatively with her. Still, having done so, I felt that an acknowledgement of my role was needed. Thus I stated: "You and I have become involved in a mutual teasing, which I have obviously enjoyed, and I imagine you have, too. But in so doing, I think that I have repeated with you, without actually having sex with you, some of that sexually provocative play that took place between you and your brother." This acknowledgement was fully accepted by B. In the following weeks, not only did she reveal further aspects of her history, but as we gave up the mutual provocativeness, her depression and anger became overt. This lasted for a long period. The sexual fantasies on my side, and on hers, were relinquished. Eventually, with the working through of the depression, a nonsexualized sense of warmth developed and maintained itself, for the most part, until the end of the treatment.

The Phallic Character

The nosological label *phallic character* or *phallic narcissistic character* has been employed in various ways by various investigators. The classical position, with its focus on libido theory, has been to see the phallic character as someone, male or female, who is fixated at the phallic level of psychosexual development. This stage is judged to begin at about 4 to 5 years of age (Fenichel 1945), or even at 3 years of age (Nagera 1975). Largely due to shifts in libido from anal to phallic concerns, it is argued, the boy concentrates on his penis, and his principal fear is one of damage to that organ—that is, castration anxiety. Similarly, the girl concentrates on her clitoris, her penis equivalent, and she struggles with both her sense of being castrated and her penis envy. Other investigators have sought to deemphasize the phallic aspects of the phallic character, and instead have stressed the narcissistic features of this type of patient. This is especially so recently, with the surge of interest in narcissism and narcissistic character pathology. Here the emphasis is placed on the phallic character's self-pathology, narcissistic deficits, and narcissistic defenses, including his or her phallic character traits (Eber 1981).

While differing in their underlying metapsychological assumptions, both classical and nonclassical approaches tend to agree as to the expectable behavior and type of characterological traits that are assumed to be found in phallic characters. Both approaches thus stress that in phallic characters one sees the following: in males, a pronounced, even swaggering, assertion of their masculinity; and in females, an exaggerated form of assertiveness that is infused with aggression, with a corresponding derogation of their more typically feminine traits. Passive and dependent longings are eschewed. The classical position views the disavowal of this passivity and dependency on the part of both male and female phallic characters in terms of a rejection of unacceptable, passive-feminine strivings. The nonclassical position, emphasizing self-pathology and narcissistic features, sees the defense against passive-dependent longings primarily as a defense against the narcissistically threatening nature of these longings.

What kind of sexualized countertransference might be expected to develop in the male therapist who is treating a phallic character? In my observation, the sexualized countertransference is similar, although with some variations in emphasis, whether the patient is male or female. Two facets of this countertransference are particularly worthy of note. The first stems from the patient's wish to be seen as highly potent and forceful—more potent, in fact, than the therapist. The therapist's position as an authority is envied by, and threatening to, the phallic character. The patient frequently engages in a form of phallic jousting with the therapist, attempting to demonstrate that the therapist is not so potent and enviable after all. The therapist's observations and interpretations are parried, or if accepted, they are embellished by the patient. The phallic character almost always needs to have the last word and must be the ultimate authority.

Confronted by such a patient, the therapist will experience in some measure the patient's wish to castrate him, not only in the literal sense, but also in the sense of robbing him of his potency and effectiveness. The danger here is that the therapist will fight back—for instance, by becoming competitive with, or even "castrating" of, the patient. At the other extreme, there is the danger of the therapist's becoming overly submissive to the patient. Parenthetically, it might be added that those therapists who by disposition and intellectual persuasion have gravitated to Kernberg's recommendations (1975) for treatment of narcissistic personalities are more likely to err on the side of taking up the joust with phallic characters. Correspondingly, therapists who are disposed to Kohut's

(1971, 1977) view are more apt to err on the side of excessive submission. Be that as it may, the therapist must certainly become aware of and work through his induced sense of being robbed of his masculinity and effectiveness.

A second, and related, facet of the sexualized countertransference to phallic characters stems from the passivity and dependency against which these patients are so stringently defending. For the female phallic character, the passive-dependent longings threaten to expose her to narcissistic woundedness and humiliation. She fears her underlying wishes to lean on another person, especially inasmuch as these wishes are directed toward a man. She dare not be passive with a man; to do so would make her feel weak and feminine. Indeed, in her lexicon, the very notion of femininity carries with it a sense of frailty. She therefore attempts to get the therapist to play out the passive role while she, the phallic one, takes over.

> With one female phallic character, I recall having fantasies of how she would seduce me, and in so doing, she would be the one who directed the scenario. As it became elaborated, she was clearly the one with the power, the one with the penis. I was passive and she possessed me. I experienced this with some excitement, but also with a sense of being had. It was my awareness of this fantasy that gave me a most poignant sense of what she, in her phallic armor, was vigorously attempting to fend off: To be passive and dependent with me, a man, was ultimately a humiliating act.

For the male phallic character there is a similar equation between his passive-dependent longings and a sense of frailty and femininity. In addition, this feeling of weakness is typically accompanied by homosexual feelings. The homosexual wish usually takes the form of a desire to be penetrated by the powerful therapist. All of this is defended against by the patient's projectively identifying these feelings in the therapist. Hence, as with the female phallic character, I have experienced the fantasy of playing the passive partner, of being the one who is possessed. I recall one patient with whom I constantly struggled with a temptation to boss him around or, more subtly, to give him advice about how to lead his life. It was not until I began to experience—first in a dream and later during the sessions—a wish for passive sexual contact with him that I was able to come to grips with the resistive nature of my bossiness. I was then able to begin working through the induced sexualized countertransference.

The male phallic character's defense against homosexual longings will occasionally manifest itself in a recitation of his sexual exploits. Again, awareness of one's sexualized countertransference is helpful.

I remember working with one young man who defended against his passive, homosexual longings with a pronounced Don Juanism. He would often recount his tales of seduction in great detail; as he did so, I would sometimes find myself becoming sexually aroused. It became apparent that part of the unconscious aim of his storytelling was in fact to do just that—to arouse me. Under the guise of a "macho" sharing of his sexual prowess, we were to engage in a mutually exciting homosexual sharing, as well as a form of misogyny, the aim of which was to preserve his powerfulness and maleness, as well as mine. Only

women were weak and frail. My sexual excitation
made me aware, however, of the frailty that he both
denied and feared—namely, the longing for homosexual contact with me.

Disclosure of
Sexualized Countertransference

A difficult technical question is what, if anything, can be
usefully disclosed of the sexualized countertransference. I
can offer only a brief observation or two.

In principle, it would seem that if one selectively
discloses other countertransference experiences (such as
anger, boredom, or withdrawal), so also would it be logical
to reveal, at times, sexual feelings and fantasies. In practice, however, I have not found that the disclosure of
explicit sexual fantasies and wishes has ever proved helpful. On the contrary, on the three or four occasions when
I have done so, I have felt my disclosure to be detrimental
to the treatment. The patient seemed frightened or enticed, which in turn temporarily short-circuited or unduly
intensified the sexualized transference, or caused the patient to transfer his or her sexual aims to another person.
There seems to be something in the revelation of this
material that is inherently overwhelming, much as the
disclosure of serious wishes to strike or harm the patient is
also almost certain to prove overwhelming.

The question of whether it might be helpful, on
occasion, to reveal sexualized countertransference in a
nonexplicit, generalized manner (for example, "attrac-
tion" to the patient) is one I cannot answer with confidence. My few attempts to do so have led me to be some-

what skeptical about the usefulness of such disclosures. The sole exception is in those circumstances (as with my masochistic patient, B.) when both the patient and I have become aware that we have been enacting aspects of our sexual feelings toward each other. Then, and only then, have I found it useful to make a *general* statement about my countertransference. Thus, with B., I acknowledged my "enjoyment" of our sexual bantering, while indicating that for the sake of the treatment we needed to halt this resistive pattern. I believe the treatment would have been better served had I not enacted aspects of the sexualized countertransference; yet, having done so, my open acknowledgment affirmed B.'s belief in my genuine and overriding commitment to help her. I might add, though, that I most likely would not have revealed any aspects of my sexualized countertransference had I not become caught up in enacting these feelings.

At this point I am inclined to be chary of anything other than a limited use of disclosure of sexualized countertransference. However, the "silent" use of these feelings and fantasies, as a source of information about the patient and the ongoing transference-countertransference matrix, is one that in my view is demonstrable and undeniable. While I have found it useful to employ nosological categories, it is important to reiterate that individual differences certainly do prevail within any category. Generalizations can be helpful, yet they should not blur the unique characteristics, including the transference characteristics, of each patient.

Similarly, there are differences among therapists. As Racker (1957) has pointed out, each therapist must be aware of his "personal equation." He must be familiar with those countertransferential situations in which he is likely to be most evasive or impelled to act out. A knowledge of general and expectable countertransference possibilities is simply a place from which to start. This chapter is an effort in that direction, an attempt to demonstrate that an awareness of sexualized countertransference can be valuable both as a means of knowing the patient and as a way of eliminating subtle forms of evasion and acting out. As therapists continue to focus on the technical importance of countertransference in general, the specific domain of sexualized countertransference will need to be explored further.

—— 6 ——

Countertransference with Suicidal Patients

Nearly every therapist comes across a number of patients who threaten, or actually attempt, to commit suicide. In treating such patients the therapist must manage many difficulties, not least of which are his countertransferences. The first part of this chapter is devoted to several of the countertransference problems that occur in the treatment of suicidal patients. The second part explores from a countertransferential perspective some of the principal issues involved when a patient does commit suicide—in particular, the therapist's struggle to mourn the loss of the patient.

Before discussing some of the specific countertransferential problems which may arise in the treatment of suicidal patients, it is worth mentioning two general issues regarding the treatment of these patients. The first point pertains to the overall therapeutic stance of the therapist vis-à-vis the patient. Several investigators have emphasized that the threat to commit suicide is a "cry for help";

thus, as part of the technical management of the crisis, therapists frequently need to become more active with their patients than they normally might be (Farberow 1970, Kobler and Stotland 1964, Litman 1970, Tabachnick 1961). It has been pointed out that therapists may have to recommend or insist on medication and hospitalization, and they may need to enlist direct support from other family members. Furthermore, therapists also often need to become more verbally active with these patients, sometimes openly advising and consoling them. To this list of activities, I would also add another form of activity, one which is more germane to this chapter: the necessity, quite often, for therapists to become immediately and directly open with these patients about countertransferential reactions to them and especially to their suicidal thoughts and wishes. I am inclined to believe that therapists are more likely to err with suicidal patients by remaining passive and hidden than by becoming active and revealed. Such revelations of self *can* create difficulties, or "parameters" as Eissler (1953) called them, in the further treatment of such patients. But in the management of a suicidal threat or crisis, it is often advisable for therapists to so disclose and expose themselves. In some of the clinical vignettes presented in this chapter, I will clarify what I have in mind by this type of countertransference disclosure.

Another vital issue in the treatment of patients at suicidal risk is the therapist's point of view regarding the acceptability of taking one's own life. This is an issue of considerable complexity, involving the therapist's "personal equation" (Racker 1957), as well as his ideals, values, and *weltanschauung*. The predominant view among researchers is that the therapist's job is to keep the patient alive. As Litman puts it, "At moments of crisis, the psychiatrist must be able to throw his weight into the balance on the side of survival" (1970, p. 406). A minority view, expressed some years ago by the existential psychoanalyst Binswanger (1944/1967), is that at times the therapist must accept the inevitability and appropriateness of the patient's wish to die.

It is beyond the scope of this chapter to tackle the philosophical and moral issues underlying these perspectives. Suffice it to say that while in principle I believe that for some patients suicide may be an appropriate course of action, in practice I have not yet treated a suicidal patient for whom an immediate ending of his own life seemed (to me) to be the most sensible course of action. I invariably have found myself thinking, and often saying, "Death will always be available if needed, but in the meantime let us wait and see what we can do." In short, I find myself throwing my weight behind survival.

My point here is not so much to argue for a particular philosophical perspective, but rather to indicate that each therapist is bound to have a personal outlook on the issue of suicide, and that this outlook is likely to enter into the treatment of these patients. The danger of holding the view that suicide may be an appropriate course of action is that this view can become a self-fulfilling prophecy, especially if it becomes harnessed to the therapist's unconscious countertransferential wishes to rid himself of the patient. On the other hand, when the therapist holds the opposite conviction—that suicide is never an appropriate course of action—he may find himself malignantly out of touch with the patient who is convinced that it is the right course for him. This is especially possible if this conviction is employed by the therapist as a shield against induced feelings of hopelessness and despair. In sum, what is required of therapists is a familiarity with their own

philosophical perspectives on suicide, as well as an awareness of when and how these perspectives may impinge on
their interaction with particular suicidal patients.

At this point, let me turn to some of the more specific
countertransference reactions that arise in the treatment
of suicidal patients, including (1) withdrawal and disconnection, (2) aggression, (3) omnipotent concern, (4) hopelessness and despair, and (5) jealousy of the patient's
"lover," Death.

Withdrawal and Disconnection

Of the various countertransferential states that may arise,
the therapist's sense of withdrawal and disconnection
from the suicidal patient is perhaps the most ominous.
What makes this development all the more insidious is
that, by its very nature, it often escapes the attention of
the therapist: In his withdrawal from the patient, the
therapist loses emotional interest in the very fact of the
disconnection. The patient remains isolated in his desperation, ripe for a final act of desperation.

It was during my year as a psychology intern at an
outpatient mental health clinic that I first became
tragically aware of this type of lethal development. As
part of the training, each week I conducted three
intakes, or initial screenings. I had already conducted
about 60 screenings when I met with D., an extremely short, wiry, and sullen young man who
throughout the interview sat in the chair huddled
into himself. It is this image that stays with me today.

I remember few of the details of D.'s life, which
is perhaps not surprising given the passage of time.

But the truth is that even shortly after I saw D., I could remember few pertinent details. My write-up, which we reviewed after D.'s suicide, was terse and as lacking in information as D. had been during the interview. I noted that he was distant and depressed, and that at some time in the future he might be a suicidal threat, although I stated that he did not seem dangerous to himself at the moment. What I did not note, because I did not understand it until later, was that D. had become pathologically cut off from his own will to live; and unknowingly, I had become similarly disconnected from him or, more precisely, from that part of his ego that did wish to survive. I therefore did not, indeed could not, talk to the part of D.'s ego that wished to live. I did not tell him that I saw him as potentially dangerous to himself. I just let him be. I wrote up the intake promptly, handed it to the secretary for typing, and penned his name on the list of intakes I had completed so far. Some days later, after I heard the news that D. had committed suicide, I noticed something odd about my list of completed intakes. Of the 60 or so names, all were legible except one. D.'s name was written so faintly that it was virtually illegible. I realized then that the handwriting was there on the wall, but I had come to read it too late.

Since that experience with D., I have become aware that disconnection from the suicidal patient is not at all uncommon. In discussions with supervisees and colleagues, as well as in my own continued work with suicidal patients, I have been impressed at how often the therapist is prone to withdraw, at least temporarily, from his desperately ill patient. Other investigators have commented on this phenomenon, pointing out that the therapist's disconnection from the patient often precedes an actual suicide attempt (Bloom 1967, Hyland 1978, Tähkä 1977). There are several possible causes. In some instances, the therapist's withdrawal seems to be a function of his wish to avoid certain anxiety-laden feelings—despair or anger, for example; or, the withdrawal may in fact be an expression of these very feelings. In other cases, however, the therapist's wish to withdraw seems to issue not principally from his own personal conflicts (or subjective countertransference), but mostly from the patient's subtle attempts to engender this sense of disconnection (or objective countertransference); in other words, the patient, in a deadly manner, unconsciously sets out to induce within the therapist a pathological lack of concern for him, the patient.

In his edifying paper on projective identification, Ogden (1979) mentions Tähkä's observation that prior to a patient's committing suicide, the therapist often experiences a profound lack of concern for the patient. Ogden notes that this observation "can be understood as reflecting the patient's attempt to induce in the therapist his own state of total lack of caring for himself or his life. This could be viewed as an attempt on the part of the patient to: (1) Rid himself of this malignant absence of concern for life. (2) Make himself understood by the therapist by inducing the feeling in him" (pp. 359–360). As Ogden views this phenomenon, the patient engenders within the therapist that part of his ego—or, more precisely, his self—which unprotectively disregards the patient's own survival.

There is a further way of conceptualizing this phenomenon that posits specific genetic and historical factors: By inducing a lack of concern in the therapist, the patient repeats a specific transference pattern that arose out of a destructive relationship with a pathologically disconnected parent. In object relations terms, the patient choreographs for the therapist the internal imago of this uninvolved parent, who destructively withdrew from him in time of need. The schizoid past is relived in a schizoid involvement with the therapist. Unless the therapist can catch himself as he is drawn into this transference-countertransference matrix, the patient is in dire straits.

How might the therapist catch himself? Fortunately, I can report an instance in which I was able to digest this experience in time to be useful to a suicidal patient.

A man in his mid-thirties, C., appeared for an initial screening at the clinic, with the presenting problem that "life had no joy or meaning" for him. When questioned about suicidal intention or ideation, C. reported that he had no such thoughts or plans. As the interview progressed, however, it was clear that he was in a despondent state—working in a job he demeaned and living alone, with few friends or social contacts. Woeful as his situation was, I nonetheless found myself, as with D., filled not so much with concern as with a profound sense of detachment. It struck me that I did not care what happened to him.

Alerted by this countertransferential detachment, I began calling attention to *his* detachment. I suggested that in spite of his distressing situation, something in his mood indicated that he had reached the point where he did not seem to care much what happened to himself. C. agreed, stating that he had run out of energy. I then confronted him with an observation: "In having run out of energy and not caring what happens to yourself, you might be in some danger of harming yourself, if only accidentally." And I added: "You really never thought of just ending it all in some quick or careless way?" It was then, at last, that C. admitted how, during the previous week, he had found himself driving on the expressway at 90 miles an hour and had almost had an accident. At that point, I emphasized to C. that he was indeed in considerable danger, and that I would arrange for him to begin treatment immediately if he so agreed. He accepted. Months later, I was informed by the therapist treating him that C., who was stabilized by then, prior to treatment had harbored a plan whereby he would destroy himself while intoxicated by driving his car into a wall on the expressway.

Aggression

Therapists have been aware for many years that the patient who threatens or actually attempts to end his own life, may be enacting the aggressive wishes of others who would like to be rid of him. These others may include the patient's family and friends or, in the treatment situation, the therapist himself (Asch 1980, Hyland 1978, Litman 1970, Maltsberger and Buie 1974, Meerloo 1959, Menninger 1938, Richman and Rosenbaum 1970, Tabachnick 1961). The suicidal patient may be an "innocent" victim of the aggression of others. Or rather—and quite often—he may unconsciously and masochistically set out to evoke their aggression and wish to be rid of him, thus inviting them to commit "psychic homicide" (Meerloo 1959) or to act as a "hidden executioner" (Asch 1980).

There are a variety of means by which the suicidal patient may evoke or provoke the therapist's aggression. The patient can incite the therapist by acting in a blatantly demanding fashion, beseeching him for special care and consideration at any time of day or night; yet nothing that is said or done is satisfying to him. Or, the patient can thwart and irritate the therapist in more covert fashion; for example, by withdrawing from him and deflecting the therapist's efforts to reach him. What makes all this even more exasperating is that the suicidal patient, knowingly or not, often employs the threat of suicide as a means of prodding or punishing the therapist (Asch 1980, Meerloo 1959, Tabachnick 1961). The therapist is thus caught in a countertransferential bind: He is predictably angry with the patient and may wish to be rid of him, yet he is likely to feel intimidated and frightened lest any leak of this aggression cause the patient to end the treatment with guillotine-like swiftness.

The literature on the treatment of suicidal patients and, more broadly, on the treatment of borderline and psychotic patients (Kernberg 1975, Searles 1965, 1979, Spotnitz 1976, Winnicott 1949) has made clear the importance of the therapist's recognition and management of countertransferential aggression. In general, it can be said that the greatest danger to the patient is not the therapist's aggression, but his lack of awareness of such underlying feelings.

Maltsberger and Buie (1974) outline in illuminating detail some of the ways in which the therapist with a hate-inducing, suicidal patient may attempt to defend against this hatred. For example, the therapist can turn the hate against himself, thus feeling a sense of hopelessness and helplessness; or he can turn hate into its opposite in a reaction formation, thereby approaching the patient with anxious solicitude; or he can enact the hatred by subtly withdrawing from the patient or attempting to impose untenable controls over his behavior. The correct technical approach, in the view of Maltsberger and Buie, is for the therapist to "gain comfort with his countertransference hate through the process of acknowledging it, bearing it, and putting it into perspective. Guilt then has no place in his feelings, and the therapist is free to exert a conscious loving self-restraint, in which he places a higher value on the emotional growth of his patient than he does on his own tension discharge. At the proper time, the patient can be shown how his behavior leads to an attacking or rejecting response in others" (p. 632).

While essentially agreeing with Maltsberger and Buie on the "silent" use of countertransferential hate in the treatment of suicidal patients, I also believe that there are occasions when the therapist may productively disclose aspects of his hatred to the patient. One such occasion is when the therapist inadvertently enacts this hatred. At times, the patient will point out the enactment directly, or indirectly (such as in a dream). At other times, the therapist will simply notice this enactment himself (see Tabachnick's candid discussion [1961] of how he realized he had sent a suicidal patient for electroconvulsive therapy [ECT] as part of his rejection of her). When an enactment has occurred and is understood by the therapist, it is sometimes helpful to acknowledge and, up to a point, discuss what happened. In so clarifying his aggression, the therapist may open the way for a fruitful discussion of the patient's role in eliciting this aggression, which may have been less possible without such disclosure (Little 1951).

There are also occasions in the treatment of some suicidal patients when the therapist may find it useful to disclose his countertransferential aggression even if he believes he has not (yet) enacted it.

A woman patient, N., with a history of previous suicide attempts—one while I was treating her— greeted the initial announcement of my pending vacation with veiled threats that "something" might

happen to her while I was gone. A week before I left,
this "something" became a clear threat to overdose
again on sleeping pills. She acknowledged her anger
at me but had little sense of how she was blackmailing
me. For my part, I was angry with N., though at the
same time concerned that she might be in some
danger.

In most instances I would simply have processed
my reaction "silently," perhaps making an interpretation of how my pending departure had made the
patient feel I did not care or was uninvolved. With
this borderline woman, however, I sensed that a dem-
onstration of my "goodness" would only have made
her feel worse (no doubt bringing forth her "badness" in the form of additional anger). So instead I
chose to bring into the open *my* badness—that is, my
anger at her. "I'm sore at you," I told her sternly.
"What do you mean by threatening me with suicide?
Can't I go away for a few weeks without your destroy-
ing yourself and all we've done together? Look,
you've simply got to try to hold it together until I get
back!" The effect of this disclosure of my anger (and
underlying concern) was, I felt, immediately salutary. N. did upbraid me some for being angry with
her, since she was the one who was being "abandoned," but her reproach now had a calm quality to
it. We talked about how she would handle an emer-
gency when I was gone, and she agreed to take a
colleague's telephone number. I left for vacation
some days later with a sense (accurate, as it turned
out) that my patient was not in danger.

In retrospect, I am inclined to believe that my disclosure of aggression toward this patient accomplished at
least three purposes: (1) It made her, on an unconscious

level, *less* paranoid about the impact of her aggressive maneuvers toward me; (2) it rendered her less envious of my "goodness," and therefore less consumed with a sense of her own "badness"; and (3) it allowed her to feel my involvement with her at the very time when she feared I was uninvolved and about to abandon her. This form of disclosure—in a sense, a controlled enactment of the countertransferential aggression—must be employed judiciously and only infrequently. My point is merely that with some suicidal patients it can prove helpful.

Omnipotent Concern

By the phrase *omnipotent concern*, I have in mind a certain countertransferential disposition that sometimes comes into play in the treatment of a desperately ill patient, wherein the therapist finds himself determined to rescue the patient, sometimes in spite of the patient's vocal wishes to do himself in. The therapist finds himself involved in an omnipotently concerned manner, as the patient presents himself as desperately and impotently helpless. I think that this type of transference-countertransference matrix occurs for two reasons: (1) The therapist escapes into omnipotent concern in order to evade his own futility or anger at the patient; and/or (2) the therapist is pressured by the patient to enact the role of all-powerful, parental rescuer.

In discussing this type of countertransferential response to suicidal patients, some investigators are inclined to stress its function as a reaction formation against the therapist's aggression toward the patient (Maltsberger and Buie 1974, Meissner 1977, Searles 1979). Searles states this view with his usual eloquence:

And the suicidal patient, who finds us so unable to be aware of the murderous feelings he fosters in us through his guilt- and anxiety-producing threats of suicide, feels increasingly constricted, perhaps indeed to the point of suicide, by the therapist who, in reaction formation against his intensifying unconscious wishes to kill the patient, hovers increasingly "protectively" about the latter, for whom he feels an omnipotence-based physicianly concern. Hence it is, paradoxically, the very physician most anxiously concerned to *keep the patient alive* who tends most vigorously, at an unconscious level, to drive him to what has come to seem the only autonomous act left to him—namely, suicide [p. 74; italics are Searles's].

The problem with conceptualizing the therapist's attitude of omnipotent concern merely in terms of a defensive reaction against hostility toward the patient (that is, subjective countertransference) is that one can obscure or overlook the role that the patient frequently plays in engendering this reaction in the therapist (that is, objective countertransference). Transferentially, the desperate and self-destructive patient will often attempt to create an all-good parental object without which he feels, consciously or unconsciously, he cannot survive. As has been reported elsewhere, the suicidal threat or attempt may issue from the patient's fantasy of being magically rescued by an omnipotent protector (Jensen and Petty 1958). The patient sometimes attempts to induce the therapist to enact this role by obviously desperate behavior. But just as often, and perhaps more effectively, he will attempt to pressure the therapist into the role of rescuer by disregarding his own safety, while at the same time subtly providing cues that he wishes to be saved. In such circumstances, if the therapist is in deep emotional contact with the patient, he is likely to feel that he is called upon and wants to rescue the patient.

The danger here is not that the therapist at times experiences omnipotent concern and determination to rescue the patient, but rather that he gets caught up in this countertransference experience and is unable to put it into perspective because of his own excessive narcissistic needs to be in such a position with another. When this happens, the therapist is apt to prolong or invite the patient's desperation, perhaps with destructive consequences. The patient, for example, may then be driven to increasingly dangerous behavior as a way of further testing the therapist's omnipotence or, alternatively, as a way of setting up the therapist (and himself) for an ultimate act of toppling the all-powerful figure he has sought to create. In the latter scenario, suicide becomes more than an act of autonomy, as Searles suggests; it becomes a violent and self-defeating reversal of roles: The patient seizes power, and the therapist is at last rendered impotent.

It therefore becomes crucial in the treatment of suicidal patients that the therapist refuse to play out the role of omnipotent protector to a powerless patient, even though inwardly he may sometimes be tempted to do so. The therapist must inform the patient that he cannot keep the patient alive unless the latter finally wishes to be alive. Occasionally, I am inclined to add—when it is true—that as much as I *do* want to rescue the patient, I simply cannot without his help. With some patients, one may have to demonstrate one's inability and refusal to accept the role of all-powerful rescuer by calling for the help of other people in the patient's environment, or by urging hospitalization for a period of time. These are difficult decisions to make because the patient is likely to experience such actions as rejections, regardless of how tactful and accepting the therapist is. Nevertheless, it may be the only way to convince some patients that one's powers are, alas, those of a therapist and not a god.

Helplessness and Despair

Treating the suicidal patient can be enormously depressing for the therapist. As the therapist struggles to alleviate the patient's sense of desperation, he may find himself slipping into a mood of helplessness and despair, sometimes accompanied by gnawing feelings of self-doubt and guilt. Obviously, if not understood and managed in time, this type of countertransference is potentially destructive to the patient and to the therapist.

Investigators who have discussed the emergence of depressive countertransferential reactions in the treatment of suicidal patients have tended to view such reactions in terms of the therapist's defense against aggression toward the patient. Simply put, the therapist hates himself instead of hating the patient (Maltsberger and Buie 1974, Meissner 1977, Zee 1972). This formulation, which reflects Freud's original conceptualization of depression (1917), would seem to apply in many instances, particularly when guilt is an important aspect of the countertransference experience. What is required of the therapist, then, is to come to grips with his own underlying aggression toward the patient and to therapeutically manage this aggression.

The therapist's countertransferential depression need not necessarily be a defensive reaction, however. Rather, it may be an expectable, and potentially useful, response to the patient's efforts to induce such a reaction. The patient, mired in his desperation, seeks to draw the therapist into the mire with him; and he does so not just to sully the therapist, but in an effort to get someone else to know just how bad he feels. Viewed in this light, the therapist's refusal or inability to react depressively—in his *internal* experience of the patient—can be a resistance to making deep emotional contact with the patient. Parenthetically, it might be added that therapists who are most comfortable with their countertransferential aggression toward patients sometimes seem to slip into this aggression as a *defense* against the patient's depressive undertow.

As a somewhat unusual example of the way in which a suicidal patient may induce a sense of immobilizing despair in the therapist, I am reminded of an experience reported to me by a colleague.

> The patient was a borderline woman who had a history of self-destructive acts, although she had never made a clear suicide attempt. During the treatment, however, as the patient began to recall her chaotic early life, she started to ruminate about suicide. The therapist was not sure how serious these ruminations were until one session during which the patient was *not* ruminating about suicide, and yet the therapist suddenly began to experience an acute countertransferential state. She began to grow physically cold, her limbs turning almost numb. The room felt stiflingly enclosed, coffin-like. (The patient had said weeks before that the cork panelling on the walls had reminded her of a coffin.) My colleague felt a desperate sense of immobilization, as if Death were settling like a fog within the room. She quickly reasoned that the patient herself must be experiencing this state, un-

consciously or preconsciously, and in a subtle but forceful way projecting it into her. Intuitively, she decided to disclose the countertransference. The patient thereupon revealed, in a calm and eerily unfrightened manner, that she did indeed feel close to Death, and that suicide had been "drifting through (her) mind in recent days." The therapist, sensing the danger her patient was in, determined that the patient required hospitalization.

The countertransferential experience of helplessness and despair often does not occur so dramatically or suddenly, but rather descends insidiously. In the treatment of a few suicidal patients, I have found myself slowly, for a period of days or weeks, drawn into a mood of despair about the patient. During these times I have had the thought—or the conviction—that the patient was not going to survive and there was nothing I could do about it.

W., a narcissistic man in his mid-forties, came into treatment at his wife's prompting because she feared he might kill himself. The man had been in a serious automobile accident a year prior to entering treatment and had suffered a spinal injury that still caused considerable pain and left him with a slight limp. His disability made it difficult for him to continue his job as a traveling salesman, and had all but eliminated his numerous athletic pursuits. Most important, he had ceased to be a "real man" in his own eyes, with the result that his relationship with his wife, and his sexual interest, had plummetted. The man was clearly in despair. After working with W. for some months, I began to feel myself slipping into moroseness. Indeed, for a period of several weeks I found myself struggling with the sense that he was going to kill himself and there was nothing I could do about it. He had, after all, told me how he would do it: "No pussyfooting, but like Hemingway, I'd blow my brains out." I knew he had a prized rifle collection, and when I initially suggested that he give someone the key to the display room, he looked at me as if I were a traitor, a potential castrator.

I realized then that probably the only way I could help W. (he had vehemently refused hospitalization, too) was to sit it out with him. And so I did, feeling in part of my ego quite as impotent with him as he felt with his own life. In the other part of my ego, the observing or analyzing part, I knew that I could not give up on him; I could neither withdraw from him nor abandon him. In other words, I needed to manage his despair and my own. What I did during this period, then, was not to talk of my despair or his despair, but *our* despair. I told him, "We are stuck, and we have not yet figured a suitable or manly way for you to go on with life." And I added, "The rifle will always be there to blow your brains out, but if you can tolerate the pain, try to hang on and let us see if there is some way to live."

In reading these words today, I see that they do not capture what took place, nor do they explain why W. did not kill himself. In retrospect, though, I think he did not because somehow I was able to get across to him that I could tolerate his despair and my own; that I knew from the inside what his particular despair was, and that the "manly" thing to do—and yes, it was important to do the "manly" thing—was to hold on as long as there was a shred of hope. I do not think it was my hopefulness alone that helped, but the willingness to look for hope after having entered the position (to which he had brought me) of helplessness and despair. In terms of the mechanism of projective identification, what was helpful was my metabolizing the experience of despair and making a modified version available for reinternalization (Ogden 1979).

The risk—and it is a considerable one with suicidal patients—is that the therapist, having taken in the experience of helplessness and despair, then becomes overwhelmed by it. This can happen when the therapist is characterologically prone to depression or is passing through a depressing life situation. He may then be inclined to overidentify with the patient and not be able, in part of his ego, to stand back and observe what is happening. For the therapist who holds the philosophical view of suicide as occasionally an appropriate course of action, there is some danger that this view will further mire him in countertransferential despair. And if ever there were a time when the therapist does not want to impose his *weltanschauung* on the patient, this is it! In spite of the risks involved, however, I still wish to affirm the importance of the therapist's being able at times to take in the experience of helplessness and despair that the patient is seeking so strenuously and unconsciously to induce within him. For, to resist this countertransference experience is to lose both contact with the patient and probably the chance to help him.

Jealousy of the Patient's "Lover"—Death

For some patients the act of suicide becomes elaborated in fantasy as a romantic union, or reunion, with a longed-for loved one (Asch 1980, Hendin 1961, Litman 1980,

Shneidman 1973, Van Del 1977). This is a lethal development, particularly when the fantasy becomes egosyntonic.
At such times, the patient may speak in a longing or
almost swooning manner about the wish to join Death.
One patient, for example, described Death as "soft and
inviting, like black velvet." Another patient spoke of
Death as her "soul mate," who was waiting for her when
she ended this "nonsense life" of hers.

The impetus for such a romanticization of death is
almost always a wish to join a deceased loved one and/or
to recapture an imagined state of bliss with the all-good,
omnipotent mother of symbiosis. In the fantasy of death
as reunion, the patient is able to free himself of his
ambivalence toward everyone, living and dead, including
himself. He becomes purged, shedding the molt of his
worn-out life, and emerges reborn, pristine. He is no
longer excluded from the joy of being, and is finally, if
ironically, alive in Death.

In treating, or supervising the treatment of, suicidal
patients who harbor such a romanticization of Death, I
have sometimes found that a rather curious countertransferential development occurs. The therapist finds himself
competing with Death for the patient, with the conscious
or unconscious sense that he is a rival for the patient's
affections. In fact, on a few occasions I have been able to
discern that a patient of mine was falling prey to the
seductions of Death by the emergence of an undeniable
countertransferential feeling of jealousy toward whom-
ever or whatever Death represented. Twice when this
happened it was clear that the patient viewed Death as a
magical reunion with a lost relative; in one instance it was
the patient's mother, who died when she was a child, and
in the other it was the patient's wife, who died suddenly in
an automobile accident. The face of Death, then, was one

that was known, and it was clear that my jealousy was directed toward this idealized dead person who tenaciously embraced, and was embraced by, my patient. In other cases the identity of Death has been less clear (such as in the "black velvet" case), and the sensation then has been one of competing with an unknown and mysterious rival.

The therapist's chances of winning this competition are, unfortunately, not always good. This is especially so if the patient has held the therapist at arm's length, refusing to form a narcissistic selfobject bond with him. The allurements of Death are then all the more appealing. In such a circumstance, the therapist may need to hospitalize the patient immediately if he is to keep him alive. With the patient who thought of Death as her "soul mate"—a fantasy she had nurtured privately over several years—I am convinced that without hospitalization she would soon have gone off to join this beloved friend. The part of her ego that wished to survive had allowed the existence of this "soul mate" to be revealed for the first time during treatment, precisely as she was denigrating therapy and the therapist, thereby signaling the latter of the presence of a lethal competitor.

Sometimes, however, the therapist may be able to "win over" the patient by confronting him with his awareness of his rival, Death. In both cases in which the patient harbored the preconscious fantasy of Death as reunion with a dead relative, I was able to begin moving the patient closer to me and away from the grave by clarifying and confronting this lethal fantasy. What made it possible to go on working productively with these patients is that in neither case had the fantasy become entirely egosyntonic. There remained a certain skepticism about the success of such a reunion, based on a partial and occasional awareness of the imperfections of the lost loved one. Thus they were able to begin shifting their affections toward me as a potential selfobject. As this was happening, I might add, there was for me a silently relished countertransferential experience of sweet victory as I sensed myself winning out over my "rival," Death.

Coping with the Suicide of a Patient

In the remainder of this chapter, I wish to discuss some of the issues, especially countertransferential issues, that arise when a patient does commit suicide. For no matter how sophisticated our diagnostic and therapeutic tools, we cannot escape the fact that some patients do not respond to treatment and instead choose suicide. To the therapist who has been treating such a patient, this is a traumatic occurrence, a loss that must be worked through— mourned, in fact—so that the therapist can continue treating other patients, including other suicide-prone patients. In this section I will discuss, from a personal as well as theoretical perspective, difficulties I experienced after a patient of mine committed suicide. I shall also draw on material I subsequently gathered from colleagues who have also treated patients who committed suicide.

Perhaps not surprisingly, the literature on coping with the suicide of a patient is relatively sparse. Some prominent therapists, including Freud (1954) and Winnicott (1974), do mention having treated a patient who committed suicide during treatment, but neither discussed the particular case in any detail, nor did they elaborate on their reactions to the loss. In commenting on Freud's lack of discussion about his patient who committed suicide, as well as on Jones's (1953–1957) neglect in his three-volume biography of Freud to illuminate this material, Lit-